OUTCRY RESPONSE

Published by Rowman & Littlefield
An imprint of The Rowman & Littlefield Publishing Group, Inc.
4501 Forbes Boulevard, Suite 200, Lanham, Maryland 20706
www.rowman.com

6 Tinworth Street, London SE11 5AL, United Kingdom

British Library Cataloguing in Publication Information Available

Library of Congress Cataloging-in-Publication Data

Names: Davis, Kathleen, 1950- author.
Title: Outcry response : what educators need to know about sexual abuse / Kathleen Davis.
Description: Rowman & Littlefield, [2021] | Includes bibliographical references. | Summary: "Outcry Response informs and educates our educators about trauma-informed tools to promote compassion and confidence in addressing their responsibilities as mandated reporters of sexual abuse"-- Provided by publisher.
Identifiers: LCCN 2020057531 (print) | LCCN 2020057532 (ebook) | ISBN 9781475858297 (cloth) | ISBN 9781475858303 (paperback) | ISBN 9781475858310 (epub)
Subjects: LCSH: Sexually abused children--Care--United States. | Sexually abused children--Services for--United States. | Students--Services for--United States. | Child sexual abuse--Reporting--United States. | Teachers--Legal status, laws, etc.--United States. | Teacher-student relationships--United States.
Classification: LCC HV6570.2 .D38 2021 (print) | LCC HV6570.2 (ebook) | DDC 371.7/860973--dc23
LC record available at https://lccn.loc.gov/2020057531
LC ebook record available at https://lccn.loc.gov/2020057532

OUTCRY RESPONSE

What Educators Need to Know about Sexual Abuse

Kathleen Davis

ROWMAN & LITTLEFIELD
Lanham • Boulder • New York • London

To those who have experienced sexual abuse.
To those who educate, listen, respond, and report.
To those who have offended and who through support
are changing.
All are needed to stop this cycle of sexual abuse.

To those who have experienced or lost their lives to
COVID-19 or violence.

TABLE OF CONTENTS

PREFACE

We don't know what we don't know, until we know it! This phrase takes the judgement out of not knowing while summarizing the journey of trauma and healing from sexual abuse. I was in my late thirties when I accepted that I had been sexually abused. My story is in this book along with many others who have been hurt by sexual abuse. Writing this book has proven to be monumentally healing. I want to share what I have received.

I will intentionally write without reference to gender or age, the point being that survivors of sexual abuse and offenders of sexual abuse can be of any age or gender.

My hope is that the content of this book will bring understanding, compassion, and serviceable tools for those who are willing to be educated. As one person shared, there are no students or educators of any gender who are too young or too old to be affected by sexual abuse.

While touring and thanking the Unbound Houston staff for everything that they do in addressing the traumas of human trafficking, I burst into tears—tears of pain for the devastating consequences of sexual abuse; tears of joy for knowledge and skills learned. Please join me in this journey of communicating trauma-informed techniques that work.

ACKNOWLEDGMENTS

Outcry Response: What Educators Need to Know about Sexual Abuse has many participants in authoring this important book. First and foremost are the numerous survivors who have voluntarily communicated the reality of being sexually abused.

Women and men who have sought help to stop their offensive behavior have come forward to share their stories of change to integrate that hope is possible in ending the cycle of sexual abuse.

Retired and current teachers shared stories of the transitioning views educationally and socially about sexual abuse from ignoring to blaming to the significant role of mandated reporters.

A magnitude of dedicated agency personnel was involved in adding education about sexual abuse and prevention techniques. An enormity of resources is available for those who want or need support and compassion in their recovery.

Friends who have provided a multitude of feedback in the creation of this book are beyond amazing! I thank Berta for her support during the writing and publishing process.

A thanks to Ryan for his legal expertise.

All local, public library staff, especially Kim, Diedre.

For Tom at Rowman & Littlefield for suggesting the focus of educators. Also Carlie, Megan, and Karin for their guidance and collaboration.

INTRODUCTION

Outcry Response! is the title and theme of this book. An Outcry is sharing a personal experience of sexual abuse with another person. Response is how the listener replies to this Outcry. Response also references sexual abuse reporting and prevention material listed within several state department of education websites.

Our world is surviving the COVID-19 pandemic as this book is written. I note an important similarity. The term pandemic has these three major components in the definition: widespread, kills many, and is infectious.[1]

What an accurate description of sexual abuse and all abuse! *Widespread*: One-third of the Western population has reported being sexually abused. More than 80 percent of the other occurrences in the United States and throughout the world have never been reported. *Kills many*: Death is frequently the conclusion for survivors of sexual abuse. *Infectious*: Silence combined with the infectious repetition of lack of boundaries demonstrate that sexual abuse is a worldwide pandemic that needs to be addressed.

Education provides new insights. We learn by focusing on the process of listening to an Outcry, reporting an Outcry, personal healing, and global mindset. From shame, blame, denial, and taboo subject matter to awareness, knowledge, empathy, and resources, we can create a universal milieu to end sexual abuse.

Professionals of various disciplines establish trust with clients who seek education about their personal disease (dis-ease), options for care, and resources. Neighbors and friends interact frequently with friends and neighbors. *Outcry Response* will focus on educators. Any primary relationship, whether professional or personal, can lead to an Outcry of sexual abuse.

Sexual abuse can occur at any age or with any gender and usually involves an illusion of choice and the deception of shame, blame, or denial. Scenarios and survivors' stories will be described for clarity. Professionals add their proficiency and challenges while advocating for a person who has made an Outcry. A few offenders have shared their offensive thoughts and behaviors prior to seeking help to enhance or validate some prevention concepts. Many professionals locally and nationally have shared wisdom by supplying accurate information and resources for survivors and offenders. After compiling this multidisciplinary information, proposals for educators and our educational system are presented. Various resources and national hotline numbers are offered throughout *Outcry Response*.

NOTE

1. https://en.wikipedia.org/wiki/Pandemic.

AUTHOR NOTE

Recognition of Survivors' Experience

Many survivors have shared with me an Outcry of their personal sexual abuse experience, the aftershock, and recovery. Each account has a special role in the formation of this book, *Outcry Response*. Most of these survivors have never reported the sexual abuse. By merging survivor descriptions with beneficial trauma-informed techniques and outcomes, survivors will indirectly be reporting their sexual abuse while educating our educators.

Outcries, whether expressed by nonverbal indicators or verbally, will illustrate many points about sexual abuse. In the examples, an Outcry will be paired with a Response from a trauma-informed perspective. Other sexual abuse scenarios will guide teachers through the reporting process while fostering their confidence in completing a report. The post-report concerns will be noted and addressed as the focus of additional scenarios. Resources about the cited topics will be noted within the text of this book for easy reference.

The original location of the sexual abuse or the Outcry of sexual abuse from these survivors will be modified to take place in an educational venue. The purpose is to provide examples of Outcries, Responses, Reporting, and Post-Report essentials specific to an educational system or service. Another purpose is to demonstrate the numerous types of sexual abuse and how trauma-informed practices can assist the survivor and listener while in or out of the classroom. An additional purpose is to demonstrate trauma-informed methods and techniques that encourage campus-wide safety with open communication about the trauma of sexual abuse, prevention practices, and healing.

Hopefully this will expand to respectfully sharing local programs and developing national strategies that are available to all educational system locations.

DEPARTMENT OF EDUCATION PROJECT

Throughout this book, I will reference an informal project of reviewing the department of education from all fifty states, excluding the District of Columbia. The data was assimilated from a onetime search. The purpose was to view what is currently available.

This data was created by clicking on the department of education tab of each state. The next step was clicking on the search tab. Then, the phrase *child sexual abuse prevention* was entered into the search engine. All the general programs and titles from this informal research have been included within the text of this book, *Outcry Response: What Educators Need to Know about Sexual Abuse.*

The information was diverse, with some states listing a few while other states had developed an extensive resource file. A brief overview is noted in chapter 3. These entries included age-appropriate sexual abuse school curricula, programs specific to child sexual abuse prevention, information related to legislation establishing the state laws about sexual abuse, and resources for teachers, school personnel, other professionals, parents, families, caregivers, and the public.

The search of community agencies and web resources was endless, making it difficult to include everything. Many other diverse educational systems both public and private were not researched. There is a magnitude of unacknowledged resources to be explored related to safety for students of all ages. The hope is to build a resource pool nationwide related to sexual abuse reporting and prevention.

Thank you to all the people who design these websites, legal documents, programs, and resources for all our school systems and neighborhoods. AMAZING!!

I

EDUCATION—COMPASSION—RESPONSE

OPENING

Outcry is speaking out to describe, share, and express the pain, shock, and overwhelmed feeling associated with being sexually abused. Hopefully, there will be someone to truly listen and have an empathetic Response.

The Response needs to be compassionate and affirming. Compassion emanates from knowing that the survivor is not at fault no matter what. Affirming is recognizing that every survivor and listener is brave and courageous.

The sad fact is that as this book is being read more babies, children, youth, and adults are being sexually abused. Deceptive feelings of guilt and shame have impaired a high percentage of survivors from communicating an Outcry. Therefore, there are many nameless survivors living with the disturbing aftereffects of sexual assault. Anyone can be chosen at any time to be the listener of an Outcry. There is hope.

TRAUMA-INFORMED

This devastating cycle needs to stop. The combination of aftereffects from any trauma is known more officially as post-traumatic stress disorder (PTSD). Learning about how the body, mind, and soul store and transmit the damage of a devastating event is essential. Becoming a trauma-informed professional, educator, parent, neighbor, student, or community member provides hope in recognizing and releasing the anguish of sexual abuse.

Trauma-informed practices have increasingly been acknowledged as useful tools in learning how to respond and begin restoration from a sexual assault. The following are some basic concepts of trauma-informed methods and objectives as related to sexual abuse:

- learning about the complexities of being sexually abused
- recognizing the aftereffects of having been sexually abused
- educating students, families, professionals, and community members about sexual abuse prevention techniques
- facilitating concern for self and others
- establishing trauma-informed classrooms and campus-wide Responses

Trauma is defined for the purpose of this book as a life-threatening experience that effects the whole person. The body holds the trauma, which causes emotional, physical, financial, spiritual, sexual, social, and mental reactions. It is important for these reactions to be acknowledged and released to heal from this traumatic event.

REMEMBERING

During a traumatic occurrence, the survivor usually disassociates, which means that their mind goes blank. More often, a survivor will be numb while visualizing what is happening from outside of their body. Many survivors describe seeing themselves being sexual abused as if they are floating above the assault. Disassociation indirectly assists the survivor to endure during the assault.

The brain stores the feelings and the acts of violence. For a few survivors, details of the sexual abuse may be clear. Most of the time, the specifics and feelings will be accessed at later times. This process is called remembering.

Remembering can seem unbelievable because we are trained to want order. The process often occurs as triggers that are sporadic and sudden intense floods of scattered information or emotion. Triggers are reactions from stimuli that remind the survivor of the assault. These disassociated memories can "pop up" during a situation with no obvious connection. A smell, thought, word, or action may remind the survivor of the sexual abuse. There could be a sudden sense of fear or anger for no apparent reason. When triggers are not identified, the situation can be very disturbing, confusing, or mystifying for the survivor and those nearby them (i.e., teachers, parents, and other students).

If reading this explanation is confusing, think of how this must feel to the adult, child, or youth who has been hurt and has no information about this set of survival tools. This whole response often makes reporting the abuse difficult for various reasons. The survivor may not have the whole picture of what happened to them. They may have parts of the whole event in sporadic unconnected sequences. Unfortunately, this leads to a belief that the sexual abuse has not happened or doubt for the survivor and the listener.

For the observing person, the survivor seems suddenly intense or reactive in a manner that does not match the present situation. Triggers are sudden, disjointed flashes of what happened, thus mixing the past and present. When trauma-informed practices are applied, this process is more manageable for everyone.

> *What has been described is a basic summary of the protective yet confusing process of healing from the trauma of sexual abuse. Throughout this book, italics will be utilized to highlight specific trauma-informed ideas and practices. With this information, educators can respond to survivors with affirming compassion in the classroom while reinforcing a campus-wide focus on prevention for other students.*

DEFINING EDUCATORS

Educators will be defined very broadly as any person who assists in the learning process of students from birth through elders. Someone who performs educational administrative duties will be considered an educator.

Parents and caregivers at home are the first educators. Other titles of an educator may be teacher, instructor, faculty, professor, employee, educational specialist, administrator, curriculum designer, volunteer, school ancillary staff, and within this expanded definition many others.

Other examples to broaden the perspective are programs or settings such as parenting classes, technical training, treatment centers, leisure learning, English as a second language, lifelong learning, libraries, nursery school, and many others.

With COVID-19, teachers have described the sudden, time consuming, intense responsibility of finding computers for students, developing online courses and final exams, and utilizing conference calls, e-mail, and Zoom-type classrooms to facilitate learning while teachers, students, and parents are asked to stay home.

Professionals who provide services for students within schools also educate students. Some of these professionals are nurses, counselors, social workers, dietitians, agency personnel, tutors, case managers, after school program personnel, bus drivers, cafeteria staff, custodians, certified nurse aides, massage therapists, health practitioners, faith-based personnel, or ancillary teams such as office staff, physical therapy, occupational therapy, and speech therapy. Generally, anyone working within the health care spectrum and the educational system can be considered an educator.

The definition of an educator is broad to honor all our educational and administrative teams. At any time, a student survivor may choose one of these educators to listen to their Outcry of sexual abuse.

DEFINING STUDENTS

A student will be defined as a person of any age or gender who is engaged in learning. Our bodies hold the trauma of abuse and sexual abuse. Individuals including babies, persons with learning challenges, through senior adults can differentiate between someone who is calm versus someone who is agitated or aggressive. Babies begin to distinguish their families' faces from others. Persons of any age or individual learning ability can comprehend prevention techniques and how to process an abusive trauma with learning modifications and trauma-informed practices. Therefore, a student can be a baby, child, youth, adult, elder adult, or centenarian.

REPORTING PROCESS

Let us begin with educators as listeners of an Outcry. Provided will be information, support, and trauma-informed methods that shatter the damage of sexual abuse.

There is the thought that adults are knowledgeable about sexual abuse. If this is the case, what makes it so difficult for an adult teacher to respond to an Outcry? The premise that adults know about sexual abuse or prevention is one of those myths that perpetuate the cycle.

Our teachers work with students of all ages in various capacities. Because most of our teachers spend a great deal of time with our students creating a bond of support, students may choose to share an Outcry of sexual abuse. Teachers are often the first to be told, that is, first responders.

Reports of sexual abuse have been the focal point of the news while providing a multitude of information describing and defining sexual abuse for the public. With COVID-19 stay-at-home precautions, be prepared for an increase in reports of abuse and sexual abuse. Even with all the media reports and broadcasted public information, most teachers reported that they are uncomfortable with the thought of hearing an Outcry from a student.

For most teachers, the responsibility of hearing an Outcry seems enormous. Teachers reported feeling overwhelmed, at a loss as to what to say or how to fix this situation for the student.

Many significant concerns make this situation overwhelming. To start, shock is a normal reaction. Listen to the Survivor.

Teachers are concerned about the student's health and safety. Listen to the Survivor.

There are legal consequences of jail time or monetary fees for not reporting that create many potential questions. Does every comment made by a student need to be reported? Exactly how is a report to be made? Was the report completed correctly? Listen to the Survivor.

Teachers are reminded about their district or state policies regarding sexual abuse reporting and prevention. Often, this information is presented with additional items of importance. Remembering the rules can be difficult when an Outcry occurs. Listen to the Survivor.

A teacher hearing an Outcry of sexual violence might feel confused if the description changes during an Outcry. Changes in an Outcry are not unusual. Listen to the Survivor.

An employee of the local Family & Protective Services suggested *to not ask a lot of questions.* More questions will be asked by the investigation team. Just listen! Listening is the most important and effective tool of responding to an Outcry.

Debating about making a report produces another sense of being overwhelmed. The confusion about how to respond, whether to report, remembering the details, and making a report can leave a teacher paralyzed, not knowing what to do. Report what you remember. The reporting teacher is not the only source of information. A report is to be made for *any alleged or suspected* behavior.

Please do not attempt to investigate a report or make accusations. These skills are not listed in the job description of an educator. Let these investigative professionals, law enforcement, Family & Protective Services, Child Protective Services, Adult Protective Services, or other agencies in the teacher's local area do their job. The safety of a student can be compromised when others are involved.

The student survivor may strenuously object to making a report, possibly due to fear, denial, or confusion about the sexual abuse. Or the student may feel loyalty to the offender. Just listen!

When making the report, note a request by the student to not report or describe any discrepancies in the Outcry. Be honest when asked if a report will be made. "Yes, because I am concerned about your safety." If or when the survivor becomes angry, one might respond by stating "I hear that you are angry. I am concerned about your safety." If the anger becomes threatening, please leave for personal safety, get assistance, and continue by adding this occurrence with the report.

Recanting is denying or taking back the report, which happens frequently out of shame, fear, or dissociation. One may feel so embarrassed by the sexual abuse that they deny the report. They might be in fear of retaliation for breaking the secret. The survivor may disassociate and the memory slides back into the unconscious.

Teachers deserve and need accurate, clear, concise information to feel more confident and knowledgeable about defining, hearing, and reporting sexual abuse. Due to the sensitive nature of sexual abuse, an

Outcry may be missed or blocked inadvertently by a reaction from the listener.

In the situation where the listener is a survivor of sexual abuse, this teacher may be distracted while remembering their personal experience. It is normal for the teacher to experience a trigger that makes it difficult to focus on the student and the current Outcry. Please ask for help to provide for the student survivor when recognizing that the listener is distracted by their own memories of an assault. Again, we are human and are affected while listening to an Outcry.

Please listen even if the behaviors you are hearing are unusual or unfamiliar. This situation is challenging. The teacher's Response to an Outcry can be supportive or inadvertently generate shame and blame. The shocked listener may have a disturbed or distressed expression. There may be shocked responses such as "You let this person do what? How could you?" Or "Don't you know this is wrong? This will be reported." This language implies guilt and shame. The survivor who endured the sexual assault is affected by feeling responsible.

By being familiar with the different modes and patterns of sexual abuse, a teacher can be less reactive and incorporate more confidence while listening to an Outcry. Be observant and open to listening. It takes great courage to share an Outcry and to be a listener/reporter. Affirm the student for telling what happened. Reassure the survivor that the sexual abuse was not their fault.

> *Affirm the student with a "Thank you for telling me about what happened to you. I am sorry that you were hurt. This is not your fault. I am going to report this event. The person that you described did not follow the rules."*

The next step involves making the report of sexual abuse. As with all knowledge, building confidence and skills is essential related to an Outcry report. Hopefully, these scenarios will provide some basic tools.

The listening person will call 911, Family & Protective Services in the local area, Child Protective Services, or Adult Protective Services to report any alleged or suspected sexual abuse by phone. The phone line is to be utilized for immediate situations that need to be evaluated within twenty-four hours. Concern for a child who made an Outcry of being sexually abused by a family member at home is immediate.

For life-threatening situations, a call directly to 911 for emergency services is always appropriate with a reference to the Outcry. A child who is having trouble breathing, is bleeding, has severe injuries, or is having suicidal thoughts needs a 911 call. The school nurse or other personnel may be involved for first aid only. Cleaning and treatment may delete important data needed in court. Please save any cleaning materials or supplies used.

Phone calls instead of online reporting is important in situations where the survivor's safety may be compromised. Below is one brief reference to assist.

This information is for TEXAS ONLY. Other areas will have different numbers or criteria.

When do I call the Texas Abuse Hotline instead of using this website?[1]

Call the Texas Abuse Hotline when the situation is urgent. Urgent means someone faces an immediate risk of abuse or neglect that could result in death or serious harm. Call the Texas Abuse Hotline at **1-800-252-5400** for situations including but not limited to:

- serious injuries
- any injury to a child five years or younger
- immediate need for medical treatment (including suicidal thoughts)
- sexual abuse where the abuser has or will have access to the victim within the next twenty-four hours
- children age five and under are alone or are likely to be left alone within the next twenty-four hours
- any time you believe your situation requires action in less than twenty-four hours

If you need to call the Texas Abuse Hotline and are deaf and equipped with a Teletypewriter (TTY), call Relay Texas by dialing 711 or 1-800-735-2989. Tell the relay agent you need to call the Texas Abuse Hotline at 1-800-252-5400.

Call the Texas Abuse Hotline if for any reason you have trouble reporting your concerns on the website.

When one calls the number to report, the agency professional will guide the educator through the process. They will ask about the student's location on campus with the campus address, student's home address, emergency contact, parent or guardian information if underage, and other important material. Having the student's data sheet available will make this call easier.

If one does not know the answer, state "I do not know." If you are not sure, then answer to the best of your ability or respond by "This is what I heard or saw" or "I do not know the answer to that question." Provide an explanation of what the survivor said or did while talking with the listener. Add the persons named by the survivor if able to remember and any behavior involved as described by the student/survivor. Note the stated relationship between the offender and survivor if no specific names were given. Be gentle if one does not remember all the details. The survivor will be interviewed by other professionals during the investigation.

A report can be made anonymously or by identifying yourself. When the listener/reporter identifies themselves, they usually receive a return call from the agency personnel to clarify what was reported and any specific concerns prior to interviewing the survivor. An identified reporter also receives a case number. This case number can be used when calling in any additional information or to access basic information regarding the investigation. Typically identifying while reporting provides that person with more opportunities to offer pertinent information and obtain the case status.

The following are some additional suggestions for after the call, while waiting for the investigative team.

- Allow the survivor to remain near the staff in a quiet place such as the office, the counselor's office, or the clinic/nurse's office.
- Please inform the survivor that another person will be speaking with them about what happened.
- Family & Protective Services will coordinate with the reporting teacher or designated person to arrange for a visit prior to the end of school or the arrival of a parent or other family representative for an underage student/survivor.
- Ask the agency when to contact the parents, guardians, or emergency contacts. The agency may prefer the family be contacted

after the interview. Keep in mind that the student may have already made that call on their personal cell phone.

The after-report period can be an incredibly tense and critical time for the teacher and the survivor. The survivor will be confronted with reviewing the sexual abuse many times during an investigation. The teacher who knows about the sexual abuse will likely be interacting with the survivor and family for the duration of the investigation. Both situations will bring about a strong need to discuss what is occurring.

There is a temptation to discuss the incident with the survivor, the family, other staff members, or one's personal family at home. Privacy is legally binding, and confidentiality is vital for the safety of the survivor.

A referral may be added for the reporting teacher. This provides outside, confidential sessions where one can express the concerns and feelings related to reporting an Outcry. The counselor, social worker, or other professional who is trauma informed will keep records per their professional protocol. These professionals can assist the teacher in recognizing additional data that might need to be added to a report. The case number that is provided when making the original report can be used to augment information. Call the phone number provided if urgent or go online if the situation is not urgent.

The survivor may need a referral, which is usually provided by the involved law enforcement, Family & Protective Services, Child Protective Services (CPS), or Adult Protective Services (APS) agencies. The report agencies often have multiple resources for survivor needs.

When the student continues to display behaviors or feelings that are linked to the sexual abuse, a referral to a trauma-informed agency can be helpful and requested. A referral can also be made by school personnel such as the nurse or counselor.

If the case is going through the legal process, survivors and families are often told to not discuss the sexual abuse prior to a court hearing. One counselor was informed of this during a session with the survivor. This makes it difficult to provide support. Survivors need a safe place to debrief the trauma.

An official report may be investigated with the results of "no evidence of abuse found." Please remember that when another report is made in the future, the original report remains on file. This will assist in developing a case in the future.

Often, this is disappointing for the teacher/reporter. The survivor may feel betrayed and withdraw or become angry. A referral to a trauma-informed professional is always appropriate for either or both people.

Students will continue to provide clues for teachers through their behaviors, emotions, attitudes, and general responses to assignments or homework. The summary provided in this portion of the book is a brief overview of what needs to be done and how to begin. As mandated reporters, professionals are legally required to provide a report to the appropriate agency in the area. Educators are in a primary position to hear and report an Outcry of suspected or alleged abuse or sexual abuse.

Trauma-informed knowledge and practices make this responsibility more manageable. To assist in the study of these concepts, italicized scenarios will be placed throughout this book, *Outcry Response. RELAX! More will be revealed.*

SELF-CARE

Compassion fatigue is a term describing the overwhelmed feeling (fatigue) experienced by the caring person or professional. Hearing the hurtful events of an Outcry is stressful and requires understanding while acclimating what has been heard. Addressing an Outcry is considered secondary trauma for the listener.[2]

One professional who provides hope for survivors and prevention education shared that there is one common prerequisite for focusing on sexual abuse. That essential concept and practice is self-care. Self-care mends compassion fatigue.

Self-care is the answer! Before reading further, think of the ways that you as a teacher/instructor/professor/educator/employee/administrator care for yourself during the workday. Consider your self-care habits completed each evening to meet your emotional, physical, financial, sexual, social, nutritional, and spiritual needs. With a few days away from work every weekend, of course your self-care practices are a priority during this time off. An educator will be better prepared to focus on an Outcry or learn more about sexual abuse if one has daily practices of self-care.

If one finds that self-care is lacking or totally absent, the next four suggestions can assist in developing some ongoing self-care practices.

If one chooses to complete this assignment, there are no grades. Phe-
nomenal benefits can be revealed.

1. *Reread the previous paragraph beginning with the sentence,*
   "Self-care is the answer!" List random feelings or thoughts, either
   positive or negative, that occur to you.
2. *Make a list of the actions or activities that are available to you for*
   self-care with a smidgeon of fun. Consider your physical, spiritu-
   al, financial, sexual, social, nutritional, and emotional needs.
3. *Discuss self-care with those significant persons in your life who*
   are willing to listen.
4. *Design a vision of your ideal self-care practices. Be creative.*
   Write, color, sketch, cut and paste, or use your innate talents and
   skills. Self-care is vital for your survival in the world of COVID-
   19 and sexual abuse.

SELF-COMPASSION

Self-care is utilized in other settings—not during the tense moments, such as an Outcry of sexual abuse. During the Bowles Chapel Lecture Series 2021, Dr. Kristin Neff discussed the effective use of self-compassion with oneself and others as opposed to empathy to provide emotional regulation *during* a stressful situation. In her presentation *Self Compassion: Building Resilience and Enhancing Wellbeing* on January 22, 2021, she noted that empathy drains and leads to burnout, whereas self-compassion energizes and calms.

Dr. Neff noted three parts to self-compassion. The first is to recognize that suffering or pain is present. The second is the recognition that other people have pain and suffering which are normal human experiences. Another aspect is that the listener did not cause the pain or suffering. By utilizing kindness for oneself and others as the third part, calming can occur. Educators and administrators can learn to use self-compassion to enhance their ability to stay present and energized on their jobs.

NO!

Whether the person is an adult, youth, or child, survivors were not given a choice. No means NO! Not providing an answer means NO! One professional shared the experience of students learning to scream or shout out NO! during a prevention program. Next, let us explore some common misconceptions about sexual abuse.

INFORMATION ABOUT SEXUAL ABUSE

Sexual abuse is not sex. Sexual abuse is violence! The assault focuses on the sexual organs, more obviously the genitals, nipples, chest area, rectal area, and breasts. Other areas could be lips, mouth, face, or areas near these organs. Often people refer to the skin as our largest sex organ. This concept adds additional thought to the concept of sexual abuse and ways to protect oneself. No one has the right to touch another person in any way without comprehensive consent.

Because the assault involves the sexual organs there can be feelings of unworthiness or degradation. A predominant myth is one that labels our genital area, including the urinary and rectal systems, as dirty, particularly due to the function of being waste disposal sites for the body.

The whole concept of being sexual has been correlated with the term "dirty." Girls are to be innocent with no information or experience for purity. Then suddenly with a wedding, consent, or a commitment, these women are now to be comfortable and knowledgeable about all their body.

In the world of myths or false beliefs, females learn about the act of sex from others. The female is to be submissive and taught. After a sexual assault, offenders often stated that they were teaching the survivor whether younger or older what they needed to know about sex. Again, this is not education. This is sexual abuse.

If females do have experience, they are considered promiscuous, whores, or prostitutes, which are considered shameful. Unfortunately, sexual abuse is socially viewed as sex. Sexual abuse is violence, not sex. Shame and feeling dirty are major factors in not reporting sexual abuse.

Because of this dirty feeling and the injuries, most survivors want to clean themselves after being sexually abused. This is understandable but needs to wait for important reasons. A survivor usually will need to be examined by a physician or medical team. The survivor needs to be reminded to not wash or clean any part of their whole body.

An exam for sexual abuse is usually more extensive than a regular yearly well woman exam or male genital exam. This exam can be very traumatic due to injuries and the multiple tests. Emotionally, this exam usually reminds the survivor of the terror of the sexual assault.

Today, many emergency rooms or trauma units have a team of forensic physicians and forensic nurses especially trained in providing the survivor with emotional support while collecting the necessary data and specimens for legal purposes. Through the Office for Justice Programs within the Office for Victims of Crime, nurses with this special training are titled Sexual Assault Nurse Examiners (SANE).[3]

Most states have advocacy programs. A few agencies in Texas include the Brazoria Alliance for Children, Montrose Center for persons who are lesbian, gay, bisexual, and transgender (LGBT), and the Houston Area Women's Center for heterosexual individuals. Survivors have access to support during the testifying process. The Louisiana department of education website provides a reference to child advocacy.

For the survivor's health and well-being, numerous tests will be taken to screen for exposure to infectious diseases for both genders and pregnancy if the person is female. Today, COVID-19 testing will be essential which requires masks and face shields worn by the staff during this intense exam. For the survivor, feelings of being unclean or dirty maybe enhanced by these additional barriers. Treatment of the physical and emotional injuries has barely begun.

A survivor will likely need to have repeat testing after a specific amount of time to obtain clear results related to exposure to some infectious diseases. Only two states, Alabama and Washington, had a program listed for students on their websites about sexually transmitted Human Immunodeficiency Virus (HIV) and Acquired Immunodeficiency Syndrome (AIDS). The student survivor will be living with this unknown for several weeks.

One woman in her early twenties decided that marriage was the only answer. They had been sexual and shame did not allow a discussion with someone else. This person had opted one evening to be sexual out of curiosity with the young man she had been dating and considered marrying. During the experience, there was a distinct sense of familiarity and thoughts of "what is the big deal?" The other person had mentioned several times that he could marry another person in another state as incentive. This statement is a threat, which makes this sexual experience abusive while the curiosity portion is not honoring the young man involved. A minister performed a premarital session and gave approval. This woman was unable to share her doubts and walked down the aisle while not wanting to be married. Her husband requested a divorce after three years because he had impregnated another woman whom he wanted to marry. Many years later, this survivor learned of being sexually abused during her childhood.

> *From a trauma-informed perspective, both young people needed education and conversation about their behavior. For the young woman, love was demonstrated by sexual abuse. The feelings of familiarity, the exposure to threats, and the need to connect through intercourse was a reenactment of the sexual abuse. This young woman lacked decision-making skills and ignored the original instincts that said, "No, this is doesn't feel right." Her feelings of shame and confusion did not allow her to ask for information or help. In her misery, she obsessively spent hours focusing on the right wedding songs, hoping that this would make everything all right. After this marriage ended, she went on to have several sexual partners to avoid being alone. She was continuing to love in the way she experienced from the sexual abuse. This woman participated in extremely dangerous behaviors without recognition at the time. Sex addiction is described as the compulsion to connect with sexual behavior no matter what the personal consequences for self or others. Some of the consequences involved nearly getting shot, a sexually transmitted disease, sex with the friends and brothers of her partners and spending large amounts of money to dress in what she called her sex addict clothes. She became an offender by pressuring one partner several times to be sexual even after hearing a clear No! Even with all these experiences, she never had what she really wanted, self-love.*

MYTHS

In our culture, we have many myths about sexual behavior that perpetuate sexual abuse. The male is to have experience and be the aggressor. Aggression and experience just for the experience is teaching males and females to be offenders. When males or females choose to have different behavior than the described norm, they may feel that their masculinity or femininity is threatened and may be harassed or experience violence.

The male survivors were often asked why they did not fight back. One myth is that males are to fight and protect. Being sexually assaulted is a deep breach of one's ability to protect self or others. For males who are assaulted by males or during same-gender domestic violence, the assault experience is one of aggression and terror, not a fight.[4]

When females experience domestic violence within the couple or female-to-female assaults occur, one female is an offender. The other is a survivor. Often no help arrives because others believed the myth that it is normal for couples to fight or that women engaged in a fight is not dangerous, just a "cat fight." Cats die from fighting; so do humans. Again, these are assaults, not normal behavior.

During a faith-based program, the educator became aware that the teens were attempting to establish "how far can I go?" as in a contest or competition, another myth of conquest. This phrase relates to the progression of touch, starting with conversation, kissing, petting, or touching each other above or below the waist, clothes on, clothes off, to having intercourse. The teens wanted the leader to tell them when to stop to be acceptable within their faith.

> *This educational program provided an opportunity to discuss the concept of boundaries, what boundaries mean, the need for refusal skills, and the development of boundaries on a personal basis. The other option is to rely on others, especially peers or the person they are dating to make sexually related decisions.*

CLUES ABOUT SEXUAL ABUSE

A person stated that throughout the generations "we received the things we didn't need and not the things we needed." Several adult survivors summarized the childhood sexual abuse experience by noting this concept: "I would do anything. I just wanted to be loved." Another thought is "How could I let that happen?" Survivors did not have a choice and often continue to carry the shame and guilt of the sexual assault from many years ago. Survivors need to be reminded that the responsibility stops with each offender.

DIAGNOSIS

Many signs and symptoms of sexual abuse are in fact the reenactment of the sexual abuse and need recognition. The witnessed behaviors or emotions are about triggers and the remembering process, not about the mental health of the survivor.

One church has two programs: one for women survivors and another course for persons with mental health concerns. Many of the survivors are in both programs. A high percent of those attending the mental health course have had a child sexual abuse experience.

Survivors may rotate in and out of psychiatric units, hospitals, or institutions. Some state mental health institutions are beginning to include trauma-informed ideas and recognize that many people with mental health diagnoses are also survivors of abuse. The focus while in the hospitals can include mental health treatment with trauma-informed practices, therapists, and art therapy. The goal is independent living after discharge. Unfortunately, funding and staffing are often a challenge.

Some state mental health institutions have employed certified peer specialists for support in addressing substance abuse, addiction, and mental health by focusing on trauma-informed methods to support survivors. Providing a safe, supportive environment allows for those survivors having a mental health diagnosis to explore the possibility of abuse or sexual abuse and receive trauma-informed treatment.[5]

When a person is placed on psychiatric medications, the focus becomes living with a mental illness, rather than healing from the trauma of abuse or sexual abuse. One survivor shared discussing her symptoms with a psychiatrist. This professional had no clue about trauma signs. Her point was that the symptoms continued and got worse, requiring different or additional medication. There was no end to this scenario.

While seeking another approach, this survivor learned from a trauma-informed professional that these signs and symptoms will continue for a long time until it is safe to talk about the abuse or sexual abuse trauma. Our bodies hold the trauma after an assault. A survi-

*vor needs to feel safe to discuss, process, and release these traumatic
reactions.*

Many survivors have signs and symptoms from the sexual abuse that
support a mental health diagnosis. Any child, youth, or adult with a
mental health diagnosis may alert teachers to consider that this person
has been abused—physically, emotionally, financially, spiritually, verbally, or sexually.

One survivor shared the trial of experiencing the post-traumatic
symptoms of hypervigilance, depression, anger, increased activity, agita-
tion, scanning the environment frequently due to fear, and decreased
concentration. Many of these symptoms could be listed under the diagnoses of Attention Deficit Disorder (ADD) or Attention Deficit Hyper-
activity Disorder (ADHD), of which she had been diagnosed.

> *As she continued to process the trauma, this survivor learned how to
> recognize these reenacting scenarios or symptoms. There was more
> balance in the response because this survivor understood that these
> strong feelings are related to past sexual abuse, not totally about the
> present event.*

Another example is a woman becoming fearful and beginning to shake
during a pelvic exam. For some, this reaction might be considered
normal because of the embarrassment of this type of exam. Some mental health professionals would place this woman on medication for an
anxiety disorder. The behavior was an instant sign to the trauma-informed professional performing the exam that this woman was likely a
sexual abuse survivor.

Many school-based programs provide education about emotional
health as part of their curricula. Most of these programs also include
socialization skills. Three states have related curricula, according to research on the state department of education websites. The three are
Arizona with *Youth and Mental Health*, New Jersey with *Social and
Emotional Learning*, and West Virginia with *Toolkit for Connecting
Social, Emotional, and Mental Health*.

> *Becoming aware of clues that sexual abuse has occurred can be bene-
> ficial. Some signs to consider are the behaviors associated with the
> terms* seductive *or* promiscuous. *These survivors are affirming them-*

selves by using their physical shape or sexual words to encourage sexual connections with one or more partners. The offenders reinforced this misinformed connection during the sexual abuse. These terms and behaviors describe a survivor attempting to seek attention in the only way they have experienced, especially if the sexual abuse happened when they were young. We need to refocus our language and understanding of the signs and symptoms of sexual abuse.

Frequent family relocations and homelessness are circumstances that may be indicative of survivors of sexual abuse or abuse. Our homeless population normally has a high rate of survivors. Many school campuses have students and families who move frequently. Military families are often transferred. Relocating and homelessness add challenges for meeting the educational needs for survivors of all ages. Some families may make these moves without abusive behavior. These two situations of relocating or homeless families need awareness, not accusations.

Another set of clues might consist of young children portraying sexual behaviors that are normally seen in adults. Siblings who have been sexually abused often begin to reenact what happened to them with their siblings. One survivor spoke of becoming an offender by sexually abusing her brother and neighborhood children in a pattern like her own sexual abuse. Teachers and school personnel need to be aware of children sexually offending children as a sign of having been sexually abused.

Any extremes in responses can be from a trigger, something that reminds the survivor of the trauma of the sexual abuse. A student may suddenly leave the classroom. A survivor may intensely demonstrate fear, anger, or rage immediately after being quiet or stoic. These reactions are clues about the strong feelings during the assault and need to be addressed from that perspective.

Many survivors have eating disorders or frequent bouts of nausea, diarrhea, or constipation. Nausea or diarrhea to rid the body of the unwanted touch is a common reaction to sexual abuse. Constipation could be a response of holding the terror of the sexual abuse. Whether one completely agrees with these correlations, be alert to the possibility of sexual abuse history with students who demonstrate these clues.

Frequently, shame and guilt from the sexual assault are present when survivors attempt to control their eating in relation to their personally distorted body image. Teachers may need to be alert to students who speak negatively and critically about themselves. Another clue might be obsessive need for cleanliness or lack of personal hygiene.

Survivors often perceive themselves as fat because they feel that they *have no right to exist*, while others may see a malnourished person. Or survivors who are medically obese struggle to maintain a healthy body weight because of the *need for layers of protection*.

A person can utilize one or more of these characteristics of eating disorders while attempting to retain the illusion of control. This is an overview that may not recognize all types of eating disorders.

- anorexia (not getting enough nutritional intake or a loathing of food as an emotional reaction)
- bulimia (being able to eat, then proceeding to vomit to maintain their perceived body image)
- compulsive eating (inability to stop eating when nourished or a longing or craving for certain foods while eating larger quantities that never satisfy)
- excessive or unnecessary use of laxatives to release water and nutritional substances to maintain one's distorted body image
- meticulous obsessive rituals or patterns around food or eating

Another form of a self-harm ritual is self-mutilating or self-injury, often used by survivors of abuse or sexual abuse. One survivor would use objects that caused injury when being sexual with herself to change numb to feeling again. With help, she released this need. Self-mutilating means injuring oneself to counter deep feelings. This situation is often different from a suicide attempt. If the injury becomes life threatening, call 911.[6]

Some survivors may become more recluse or withdrawn, not wanting to draw attention to themselves while endeavoring to avoid being hurt again. Other survivors may dress in layers or loose clothing, attempting to protect themselves. Being reclusive may establish an opportunity for an offender. Sexual abuse has nothing to do with what someone is wearing or not wearing. Sexual abuse is violence, not sex.

Older adults can demonstrate these characteristics. Students in the lifelong learning program may dress or act in ways that have been described. They may not have the keywords or may not recognize that what they experienced was sexual abuse.

One adult woman asked me whether a person continuing to touch after a *no* during a date was sexual abuse. Yes. Any unwanted touch is sexual abuse. Education is often the clue to awareness.

Survivors of all ages need to hear that the abuse was not their fault. These comments are often helpful. "I sense that there is something disturbing you. I am here to listen. Tell me about your experience. I am sorry that happened. You are not at fault." If the offender is or might be in the survivor's life today, this Outcry needs to be reported.

The staff or other students making sexual jokes or sexual remarks is extremely detrimental. These comments encourage offender behavior and discount what happened. The survivor hears that their pain is insignificant, and they do not deserve help. These offensive comments hurt others and need to be addressed directly and stopped.

If someone is being verbally or physically abused or is verbally or physically abusive in public, there is a high chance that there is additional abuse at home. If unsure about what to say, one can speak directly to the survivor, which will let both know that someone else is present.

The state of Wyoming department of education website listed bystander mobilization as one of the skills that need to be taught to students of all ages. One aspect of mobilization consists of speaking with the survivor and asking if they are all right. Another part is telling others at the scene that this behavior is hurtful and needs to stop. Asking the others to leave disperses any audience. This is an overview of the process, tools, and skills needed to address bystander mobilization. When these skills are taught to all, abusive situations can be stopped by students or staff who are present during the offense. [7]

In a video presentation called *Mind Is Everything* on TEDx, Dr. David Hendricks discusses the relationship between increased childhood adversity (maltreatment) with the increased use of injectable drugs (addiction) and increased suicide (mental illness). The damage from maltreatment can be viewed on studies of the hypothalamus within the brain. This damage can be improved by using enhanced focus (mindfulness). The urge to hurt another (or oneself) is often the reaction of those who have been hurt. When this urge to harm appears for the person who has experienced adversity in childhood, mindfulness offers pause and can lead one to more positive, beneficial solutions.

> *Within the above information about bystander mobilization, the first mindfulness practice is talking directly to the survivor. The second is speaking directly to the crowd. Since the survivor and nearby people need to focus on the voice and the spoken information, this action can stop the debilitating dissociation and helplessness that can occur during an assault.*
> *The third mindfulness experience may happen with the offender. While focused on the speaker, crowd, and messages, the offender may recognize that the change of attention has deleted the sense of power and control and deterred the drive to offend.*

A twelve-step program called Violence Anonymous discusses ways to recover from violent behavior. Changing attention and changing location are two of seventeen tools to process or stop violent behavior. As with most twelve-step programs, there is a wealth of information for professionals on the website. To attend meetings, a person is welcome if they feel that they have the problem. The need for anonymity also provides safety to address their personal behavior; those sharing within a meeting are not to be identified. [8]

SUICIDAL

The most direct way to report suicidal thoughts or planned actions is to contact 911. Make a report of the information shared by the person. Emergency services will need the location, such as the specific address of the educational facility, what room or location on campus, and the listening teacher's phone number. Usually the emergency team will ask the listener/reporter to stay on the line until they arrive and later obtain additional information about the circumstances.

Some areas of the country have a mental health deputy who is trained for mental health emergencies. Often, the mental health deputy will be called to evaluate and refer this person to a local mental health care facility rather than jail or a hospital. One can ask if there is a special service for mental health emergencies when calling 911. [9]

Two examples of a case manager being assisted by a mental health deputy are incorporated here. The first client had spoken of ending his life. When asked how, he revealed that he had a gun behind the front door in his home where the visit occurred. The case manager indicated that there would be follow up and left the home. The case manager called for supervision and then called the mental health deputy to visit this person for an evaluation. Because the client was later released from a hospital and adamantly refused services, this case was closed. Ultimately, an adult client has the right to refuse services when they are not a danger to themselves or others.

The other client spoke Spanish, which required translation during every visit. This person reported not wanting to live, which was challenging to assess due to the language barrier. A mental health deputy who spoke Spanish arranged visits during the case management visits. The client's case was closed because their physical needs were met. The mental health deputy continued mental health visits.

Many survivors have shared about being suicidal while processing their sexual abuse. They may feel damaged, shamed, or blamed while receiving support in learning to cope. One survivor speaks of becoming suicidal at times even after years of therapy and trauma work. This person is now able to recognize and establish additional help during this time.

Suicide may be considered when a student says something global about not wanting to live. A response can open or close the conversation. Conversation stoppers are statements like "You can't do that! You're not serious?" Comments about religious views on suicide are usually not helpful at the time of someone sharing about suicide.

> An opening remark might be to state "I am concerned. Tell me what is happening for you." Listen. "What have you considered to end your life?" or "How are you going to end your life?" If their plan is immediate, call 911. If in doubt in any way, call 911.

One needs to assess personal safety while listening. If there is a weapon involved, please take care of yourself first. South Carolina and North Dakota have an active shooter resource listed under child sexual abuse prevention on their website.

Making a referral or 911 call for every suicidal thought even if the person is implying that they are OK is a helpful idea. Some people have had frequent suicidal thoughts throughout their life. They know what to say or not say to stop the conversation. This can indicate that they have a strategy to complete their plan.

Many times, the suicidal person will have a change in their demeanor from depressed to happy or content. This situation is extremely concerning because they may have their plan in place and are ready to suicide. Especially be aware if they have been giving their personal items to other people or making statements about "after I am gone."

This can be a very frightening situation for the listener. We can express concern. We can make a call for help. We can encourage conversation. We can ask if they are willing to give their life a chance. We can note that there is hope no matter what the problem. We can state that we will miss them (if you personally know them and this is true). We can let them know that if they commit suicide this is it, there is no return as they are. We can also let them know that sometimes given a spiritual intervention their suicidal attempt might not work as they planned. Then, they may be faced with additional disabilities and incapacities, whether physical or mental.

The practice of mindfulness is recognized while making the above statements when someone wants to suicide. By speaking directly to the person slowly and calmly while proposing these ideas with conversation or not, one is encouraging the student to focus and consider their decision. A contract as suggested in the next paragraph is another method of focusing the student and providing time for them to truly consider their decision.

When this survivor returns to the classroom, the teacher can provide a contract signed by the survivor declaring a commitment to not commit suicide before talking with a certain number of trusted persons who are listed with their numbers. If this contract was developed in a counseling session, the counselor can ask the student about sharing this contract with their teacher. The teacher keeps one copy; the student keeps another. Refer to this contract as needed and have suicide hotline numbers posted in the classroom or in a certain place on the campus per policy. All of these are options; there is no perfect solution or answer. By getting help for this student, the teacher has done their best.

Many state departments of education have suicide prevention programs listed on their websites. These states include Arizona, Georgia, Idaho, Illinois, Maine, Montana, New Mexico, North Dakota, South Dakota, and Washington. If your state is not listed or you are not aware of this suicide prevention curriculum, consider one of these options:

- Make a call to the district or state department of education to obtain information about suicide prevention.
- Request a suicide prevention curriculum for your class or campus.
- Ask an agency that addresses suicide for a presentation to staff, students, and/or parents.
- Get involved to see what is needed.

ALCOHOL/DRUGS

Alcohol and drugs have frequently been used prior to the sexual assault. Use increases the risk factor of sexual abuse occurring. These chemicals blur the mind. Decision making is impaired while under the influence. Offenders often use drugs or alcohol or both for the purpose of decreasing the ability to resist.

For the survivor who is attempting to blur the pain and trauma of a sexual assault, this can lead to overuse, addiction, and overdose. All can be life threatening. When the alcohol bottle or drug stash is empty, the trauma remains; thus the need for more chemicals.

When a person is addicted, craving occurs, which means the body and mind are telling the person to increase the amount to feel better. Many have lost their lives seeking this *feel better* feeling. Drug and alcohol seeking become the whole focus of life. Every decision or action is about the obsession to get more.

When speaking or interacting with an addict under the influence, one is communicating with the substance. Consequences have no meaning. Other people are of no importance. Blackouts are common with no memory of what occurred. Survivors have lost any ability to protect themselves or to evaluate the safety of a situation. People who might have considered another person's boundaries in the past are no longer able to do so.

Several states have information to educate students, parents, and teachers about alcohol, drugs, and tobacco. Following is a list programs available from state department of education websites under child sexual abuse prevention.

- New Hampshire has AOD—Alcohol and Other Drugs.
- Arizona has the AWARE program about substance abuse, mental health, and suicide.
- Illinois and South Dakota have Drug Free Schools programs.
- Louisiana has a program to report Substance Exposed Newborns.
- Nevada lists a Women's Substance Abuse program.
- Delaware addresses Addiction Education.
- Washington provides Partners in Education Join Forces against Opioid Epidemic.
- Massachusetts, New Mexico, North Dakota, Ohio, South Carolina, and South Dakota also provide education programs related to drugs, alcohol, and tobacco.

Trauma-informed scenario—classroom. Mindfulness has been noted previously and is a trauma-informed tool that helps build focus. Mindfulness means staying in the present moment while being aware of personal thoughts, feelings, and responses. As an instructor, think about the students within the class. Note any students who came to mind while reading the previous sections about the clues of sexual abuse. The previous information hopefully will give each teacher a different filter to evaluate student reactions and needs.

GUILT/SHAME

A parent later in life was informed that their adult child had been sexually abused in their teen years. This parent's immediate thought was "What did they (teen) get out of it (the sexual abuse)?" The parent explained that the teen got to use the car (implied in exchange for sex).

In this situation, the survivor was a teen. This is sexual abuse. The offender is the adult and responsible person. This displacing blame for the sexual assault is common and alerts a need to change our attitudes and thinking about sexual behavior and sexual abuse.

The parent then felt blamed for not understanding how these thoughts were blaming or shaming. Inaccurate information, myths, and stereotypes about sexual behavior and sexual abuse led to blaming the survivor or non-protecting parent, thus perpetuating the cycle of sexual abuse.

In this case, the survivor believes that they hold the power to provide sex for the use of the car at any time they choose. For the survivor, there is an illusion of control and choice. This scenario is about sexual exploitation. The adult offender is using enticement while sexually abusing a teenager. The adult offender is responsible.

The parent, as many other parents or educators, wanted to know why the survivor had not told at the time of the sexual abuse. Survivors are warned by the offenders not to tell, whether directly or indirectly by threats, injury, or enticements. With threats or injuries, there is fear of further harm to themselves or to a close person. The survivor has incorporated that they will not be believed. Often those close to them do not believe the survivor when told. The non-offending parent can have an abusive bond with the offender that blocks their ability to protect their family.

DEFINING ABUSE

Even though this book is focused on sexual abuse, all forms of abuse need to be recognized and reported. This may be a review for some readers. For other readers, these devastating descriptions may be difficult to read.

The next few paragraphs summarize a presentation from Family and Protective Services in Texas by Julie Jones, the Community Initiatives Specialist (presented March 10, 2020 at Bay Area Net for continuing education credit).

There are many types of abuse: sexual, emotional, physical, abandonment, medical inattention, and lack of supervision that are neglectful. Recently, labor trafficking and forced marriage, which are often linked to sexual abuse, have been added.

Some examples of emotional abuse include demeaning, neglecting, making threats, ignoring or abandoning, insulting, yelling, name calling, terrorizing, isolating, rejecting, or continuously criticizing.

Physical abuse consists of personal injuries or circumstances that present with a vague explanation or are questionable. A trauma-informed teacher will be alert to injuries in the mouth area or dental complaints about gum pain with torn gums or chipped or loose teeth. A student might have an overnight hearing loss, which might be indicative of damaged eardrums, or a change in eyesight from head trauma. This could be a retinal bleed that often has no symptoms. Injuries in infants or in the abdominal area for older students may be indicative of abuse. Of course, welts, loss of hair, or broken bones are suspicious. A trauma-informed teacher is alert to descriptions of accidents, extreme confinement, or cruel punishment as an Outcry from a student of any age or gender.

Neglectful supervision, neglected medical care, or abandonment are abuses that need to be reported. An official term related to parental abandonment is *refusal to accept parental responsibility*.

Physical neglect encompasses leaving a child in a car by themselves, unsanitary or hazardous living conditions, and lack of clothes, nutrition, or hygiene. For a family in poverty, lack of electricity, running water, and heat may be resolved by an alternative source without being considered abuse. CPS (Child Protective Services) or APS (Adult Protective Services) can function as a resource pool for some neglect needs. No age was approved for leaving a child at home alone.

This presentation also included information about sleep safety for infants to prevent sudden infant death syndrome. Some key components of infant safety were a smoke-free environment, infant dressed snuggly and comfortably, and sleeping alone on the infant's back with a firm mattress and a tight-fitting sheet.

The information in this paragraph was added and not in the presentation. The state of Louisiana department of education lists two programs related to infant health. They are Safe Sleep and Safe Haven. There are Safe Haven sites where a baby can be left legally if the baby has not been abused. The parent is released from responsibility. Many states have a similar program.

Another *major* concern is a parent inadvertently suffocating their infant or child by rolling on top of them while sharing a bed. This has occurred frequently enough to be noted on this presentation. This family will suffer through additional guilt, shame, and blame while grieving the loss of their family member.

School scenarios—a new baby brother or sister. For homes where abuse occurs, especially correlated with the use of drugs and alcohol, these survivors are often responsible for their siblings. During a class about babies or growth and development for older students, or step parenting or grandparenting for adults, infant care and sleep time safety could be incorporated.

Students could wrap a towel or notebook (or other object) to represent a new brother or sister to practice these new skills. There have been programs where older students were provided with an uncooked egg (baby) to live with for a time, such as one week. The "baby" always had to be with them and not broken (abused).

DEFINING SEXUAL ABUSE

A survivor of sexual abuse has not chosen to be abused and hurt. They may place themselves in this situation thinking that they are protecting others from being sexually abused. The survivors are victims of grooming or forced assault. The survivor is not at fault in any way. The offender of any age, whether male or female, is responsible for their behavior.

Sexual abuse will generally be defined as a child, youth, or adult being isolated and touched on the sexual organs of the body or spoken to about sexually oriented themes without the ability to have informed consent. Sexual abuse often occurs by offenders known to the survivor and progresses from isolating the survivor to talk to actual touching. A survivor is in no way responsible for the sexual abuse.

Sexual abuse is a devastating conquest of a survivor's mind and personal sexual space. The attack may be sudden, violent, and aggressive. Or a survivor may be exposed to constant threats and verbal abuse during the grooming process.

For young offenders, these children are likely to have been sexually abused themselves, repeating behaviors from the sexual abuse. Reporting, education, and support about other ways to interact may be helpful.

DEFINING OFFENDERS

Offenders are of various ages and any gender. Most offenders have experienced sexual abuse themselves. Violence is their only tool to release intense feelings such as fear, anger, shame, guilt, rage, loneliness, resentment, and loss. This cycle continues until the silence is broken and the secret is told. Hopefully, an Outcry from a student and a report will be the key to recovery for survivors and conceivably for offenders.

Offenders see the world and their behavior through a screen of "you caused me to hurt you." They may say, "I'm sorry," because it is expected or is needed to calm the survivor. Then with the next life crisis, the sexual abuse is repeated. One counselor who worked with sexual abuse offenders noted that some offenders laughed at the survivor for believing what they had told them.

Any crisis including COVID-19 can escalate the offending behavior. One participant in a voluntary program for offenders noted that many offenders who are new to the program are seeking help. This participant noted that there were more new persons attending in the three months of COVID-19 than compared to the prior six months. When educational institutions reopen, there will likely be an increase in noted clues of sexual abuse and Outcries. Be observant and Listen.

One agency member noted that males offending female survivors is more common. As more Outcries of sexual abuse by same-gender offenders, female offenders, and child offenders are reported, this statement may change in accuracy.

Four states, Oklahoma, Florida, Massachusetts, and Nebraska, have provided educational programs for students about domestic violence and assault on their department of education websites. The programs focus on violence during dating for teens and youth violence.

Names for offenders may range from pedophile, molester, voyeur, exhibitionist, rapist, pervert, sextortionist, perpetrator, offender, bully, rude, gangs, pimp, racist, sexist, terrorist, punk, and many more. Other names closer to home could be mother, father, sister, brother, partner, spouse, religious leader, friend, groups, community member, authority figure, or educator, to name a few.

Repeatedly, the survivor knows the offender. Sexual abuse is about broken trust and destroyed boundaries. Offenders or survivors can be anyone.

There can be actual touch, sexually related words or conversation, gender demeaning, humiliation related to one's sexual orientation, or other forms of sexual abuse. This betrayal is often very traumatic because of the switch in the offender's behavior. In front of others, the offender is appropriate, supportive, and kind. During the sexual abuse, the offender's behavior is hurtful and confusing for the survivor.

> *School based scenario—teacher offender. A trusted teacher or employee of the school often speaks with this student and assists some with their studies. Then in an isolated setting, this same trusted teacher places hands or other parts of their body on the student survivor, touching areas that are considered private. During this sexual abuse, the offending teacher is saying kind words or praise to the survivor for allowing this touch and recognizing how proud the offender is of the student for giving.*
>
> *For the student survivor, this is extremely confusing. The survivor begins to obey and then questions because the abuser has changed. The nurturing teacher is now an offending teacher. The survivor may be asking themselves, "How can this happen? I must be wrong. What did I do to cause this person to hurt me? How can the same person be so kind, then be so hurtful, with kind words?"*
>
> *Another teacher notices a difference in this student and listens to an Outcry. The listening teacher is now left with the duty of reporting an offending teacher who works at the same campus or school. The listening teacher knows this teacher and is shocked. The listening teacher may have difficulty comprehending how the offending teacher could act in such an abusive manner. The listener and the survivor may begin to doubt what happened. The survivor may rescind the Outcry while the listening teacher is confused. Often a report is not made. This scenario provides a tremendous amount of information to add to a report, such as the rescind, the shock, and the confusion. Make the report. The safety of this survivor is vital.*

Within the definition of sexual abuse as read in the opening of a twelve-step support group called Survivors of Incest Anonymous (SIA), this betrayal of a trusted person is noted because most survivors know their offenders. The betrayal related to sexual abuse by a trusted person wounds deeply, often more than the physical injuries.

Another aspect of betrayal from known offenders is same-gender sexual abuse. When a mother or female offender sexually abuses a female survivor, this adds another layer of betrayal. When a male parent or male offender sexually abuses a male survivor, this again adds another layer of betrayal. Same-gender sexual abuse is *not about homosexuality*. Remember sexual abuse is violence, not sex.

Unfortunately for a young survivor who is establishing personal sexuality, same-gender sexual abuse can compound the trauma. One survivor had been sexually abused by her mother on many occasions from birth throughout her life. Our bodies are ready to react to stimulation. This is normal. Sexual responses, thoughts, and feelings were associated with the sexual abuse, thus leading to confusion about her own sexuality and orientation.

A sexual assault can be abrupt, rigorous, and severe from an unknown offender. One survivor shared an experience of rape from an unknown offender. This attack was frightening, devastating, and occurred near home. There was no way to protect. This survivor spoke to the offender briefly after the rape and fortunately was not killed. The offender was apprehended the next morning in the same location while attempting to rape another person. This offender had murdered a person previously and had escaped from prison. Unknown offender sexual assaults, while not as high in percentage as known offenders, are more prominent than originally suspected. This occurrence is being researched to explore differences and additional prevention techniques that might help.

Sexual assault is not always about intercourse. The offender may begin by talking kindly and encouragingly while lavishing praise for the survivor. The survivor may feel important, accepted, and grateful for the attention. They now have a friend or a new relationship. If the survivor is a child, they may feel grown up, especially as subjects about sex begin. There can be gifts presented to enhance this new relationship. The myth of *The One* may begin to enter the thoughts of a teen or adult survivor who is seeking a romantic relationship.

There might be sexually related topics or conversations to commence the assault. Over time with the same survivor or survivors, the offender behavior progresses to urging the survivor to touch or be touched in private areas near or on the sexual organs.

The offender is incapable of accepting any responsibility. The offender consistently uses verbal or physical abuse with statements from their negligent mindset about how the survivor caused the violent act or sexual abuse. Some examples might be the offender telling the survivor that they were seductive, promiscuous, flirting, or acted in a certain way that made me hurt you.

The offender deflects any concerns of the survivor about the potential harm of this situation. The survivor may not trust their intuition that something is wrong or acquiesce to the abuse to deter further harm.

This slow process is called grooming. An offender is "me oriented." This is the nature of an offender.

> *Scenario—commercially exploited students. Children, youth, or adults often seek friends, companions, or relationships on the computer through e-mails or social media. The offender begins to message about similar problems. Offenders may praise and speak kindly, thus giving the illusion of a bonding relationship. The offender then meets with the survivor.*
>
> *Any questions or concerns expressed by the survivor are ignored or displaced by verbal or physical abuse on a constant basis (gaslighting) while teaching the trade of prostitution. This survivor learns the techniques and proudly becomes an offender who grooms other preteens and teens into service.*
>
> *The newest teen groomed in the "life" is arrested and now has a record with the police as a prostitute. This child is a survivor of sexual abuse. The teen groomer, while being an offender, is also a survivor of sexual abuse. This demonstrates the illusion of power and choice. Both need trauma-informed therapy. For many survivors, the journey to dispelling this illusion of power and control while discovering that they are a survivor is a lengthy process.*
>
> *The original adult offender who groomed the sexual abuse survivor into prostitution is the responsible person. Another offender is the person paying for sex with a minor. Offenders need to be held responsible and offered trauma-informed therapy.*

NON-PROTECTING PARENTS

For survivors, there is a deep betrayal from a non-protective parent, family member, or close person. These trusted people do not recognize the sexual abuse and frequently ignore or deny an Outcry of sexual abuse. Scenarios of this nature are common. A few will be presented for additional clarity.

One adult survivor shared a story of sexual abuse from her childhood. Her mother needed to go to an important event. Another attendee's seventeen-year-old son was asked to watch her child. This mother felt confident that the son would care for her daughter because the mother knew his father. Her daughter was sexually abused. This offender was asked to never return to their home, but no report was made. The offender was still open to sexually abuse other children. And the father of this seventeen-year-old offender was never told.

Today we know that this young offender will likely continue sexually abusing other children. This situation leads to many questions. Was the son's father aware of this offensive behavior and still allowed his son to sit with children? Was the son being sexually abused and repeating the patterns? A report to an official agency was needed.

Another instance of not making a report was a twelve-year-old female being fondled by her father. The young teen told her mother. This mother had been sexually abused herself for several years, hearing the message "don't tell" frequently. This "don't tell" message spanned the generations. This mother, a survivor herself, did not report the sexual abuse of her daughter.

Another survivor was sexually abused until she was a preteen by a much older brother and another male relative. When the survivor reported what happened, her mother stated that she had enticed the males. The brother reported to their mother that he was examining his sister because the other male sexually abused her. The truth is that both males raped his sister.

There was a red spot on the bedsheet that this survivor decided was grape jelly when she shared this with a friend at the time. This survivor called herself dumb as she shared this story as an adult. This woman, having no protection, was linked in shame to her abusive family. Having a prevention class might have assisted this child survivor to find a teacher or other safe adult for an Outcry.

This woman states that she does not get upset as often years later because she has been able to forgive over time. This truly sets her free. She noted that earlier after being assaulted, the offenders and her mother were oblivious to her feelings or the pain that they caused with the sexual abuse. No report was made because the non-protecting parent continued to believe that this young survivor enticed the males. This scenario is common.

One survivor described blood on the rug after being sexually abused by her drunk father. The mother, out of jealousy and anger, had the survivor clean the rug. Her mother considered her child a threat to her relationship with the father. Mother went to bed with the offender that night. The man could do no wrong. The mother was not capable of acknowledging the sexual abuse because of her own unhealthy bond with the husband. The child was three, four, and five years old at the time the above assault occurred. This pattern continued until this child entered school. Both parents had been sexually abused as children by family members.

Sexual abuse has been the norm intergenerationally within many families. These scenarios demonstrate the part that the non-protective person plays in the inner workings of an intergenerational pattern of sexual abuse. Survivors who have been sexually abused throughout their lifetime by family are often shocked when they discover that not all families abuse their children.

There is also the dilemma of denial. Sexual abuse could never happen to myself or my loved ones or the students in this classroom. The family members or teachers may have been sexually abused and are unable to talk about what happened. As noted by the scenarios, these people are often not able to inform, teach, or provide accurate information regarding sexuality and sexual abuse prevention because they did not have access to this information themselves.

The major concern is the underlying pattern of not being protected. Denial and silence add to the continuing puzzle of repeating the cycle of sexual abuse. For many survivors, this denial and silence of a non-protective person is a deeper betrayal than the trauma of the physical, emotional, or spiritual effects of the actual sexual abuse by a known offender.

PREGNANCY

Sexual abuse may include another life, that of a baby. When this occurs, the survivor now has the sexual abuse itself to process and an unborn child who can be a constant reminder of the sexual assault. This person needs support and trauma-informed counseling to add quality and peace to their lives.

Technically, here are some facts about conception, making a baby. Conception can occur prior to the first menstrual period for young females. Ovulation (the release of an egg) is first, then the uterine lining releases (period or menstruation). For pregnancy to occur, the penis (male part) can be near the vaginal opening and is not required to be inside the vagina (the female opening) for pregnancy to occur. Douching (cleansing the vaginal area) does not help in preventing pregnancy because the baby has already been created. *Douching will obliterate possible evidence of a sexual assault.*

Testing for pregnancy after sexual abuse needs to be performed for all females, especially the younger girls who have not menstruated (had a period). Children, youth, and adults deserve appropriate information on how to protect themselves and primarily how to avoid potentially dangerous situations.

Thinking that being informed will lead to early sexual behavior is another myth and adds to the vulnerability of a student being sexually abused. Sexual abuse happens at all ages. Consider two preteens who are facing pregnancy. One preteen who was pregnant at eleven years old was seen by a nurse practitioner. This new mother refused to give the name of the father. Another eleven-year-old student in fifth grade was discovered to be pregnant from sexual abuse by a family member. Both girls were faced with the trauma of sexual abuse and parenthood decisions before they have learned to adapt to puberty.

Many states in the United States now consider a pregnant teen an adult. Some women may say that "We had our babies young and did fine." The hope is to provide support for these young females, especially when they have been sexually abused, to stop this cycle.

The following states have parental programs and resources listed on their department of education websites.

- Hawaii has a variety of parenting related programs: Parent Project for parents of youth from eleven to twenty years old, Loving Solutions for parents of children from five to ten years old, Family Support Hawaii, Fatherhood program, Home Visitation program, and a parent toolkit.
- Louisiana incorporates a Substance Exposed Newborn Reporting system.
- Mississippi includes information for parenting babies and children from birth to five years old on their website.

- Nebraska lists several resources: Home Visitation program, Getting Down to Business for caregivers, and Early Learning Guidelines from birth to five.
- Rhode Island has information for families.
- Virginia lists Family Life Education.
- Wyoming includes parent information.

Our public schools are recognizing and providing helpful information and resources for parents to aid in the prevention of child sexual abuse.

CULTURE

Among the many cultures of this world, teachers are faced with the actions of children, youth, or adults who behave in ways that are defined as sexual abuse in Western culture. In some cultures, touching private areas in public is considered preparation for the child, youth, or adult to be sexual, when indeed this is sexual abuse.

> *School scenario—culture. A teacher had a young student who continued to demean and touch another student on sexual body organs in front of their classmates. The offending student arrived at the school from another country where the rules of interaction were different from Western culture. The teacher set a time for the other students to share in a non-shaming way how this behavior affected them. The student was able to understand that in Western culture these remarks and touching are offensive. The student stopped the offensive words and behaviors.*

For students in the classroom, learning about refusal skills might be a skill that stops a potential sexual abuse situation. A recovering offender recognized that the survivor had not refused. *No answer* is a No!—something that this offender learned and respects today. Refusal skills are noted to be a part of sexual abuse prevention program for the state of Utah.

> *Here is an example of refusal skills being used effectively to stop sexual abuse. The person stating a boundary stopped an unwanted hug. In this example, this person asked, "What are you doing?" when approached. This scenario was shared by a previous offender, who*

stated that this refusal ended the mind "zone" that had been present during previous sexual abusive behaviors.

One might say, "This is just a hug. What is the big deal?" The big deal is that the hug was not wanted. Any unwanted touch, approach, or suggestion is sexual abuse.

SUMMARY

From addressing an Outcry to recognizing clues to descriptions of offending behavior, a tremendous amount of information about sexual abuse has been presented. Please take time to consider your personal self-compassion and self-care practices prior to reading further.

Chapter 2 will include information from retired teachers to compare past reactions regarding sexual abuse to current-day practices and mandated reporting. Chapter 3 discusses concerns and suggestions for future utilization by educators and educational systems to promote compassion and campus-wide prevention of sexual abuse.

Trauma-informed information and practices will continue to be recognized in italics and indentation within the next two chapters.

NOTES

1. https://www.txabusehotline.org/Login/Default.aspx.
2. https://www.stress.org/military/for-practitionersleaders/compassion -fatigue; http://compassionfatigue.org.
3. https://www.ovcttac.gov/saneguide/introduction/what-is-a-sane.
4. https://1in6.org.
5. https://www.mhanational.org/national-certified-peer-specialist-ncps -certification-get-certified; https://www.mhanational.org/.
6. https://www.drugs.com/mcd/self-injury-cutting.
7. https://firsttaekwondoaz.com/2001/bystander-mobilization; https://www .nsvrc.org/bystander-intervention-resources.
8. http://violenceanonymous.org/.
9. https://hhs.texas.gov/doing-business-hhs/provider-portals/behavioral-he alth-services-providers/crisis-service-providers/mental-health-deputy; https:// www.houstoncit.org.

2

PAST TO PRESENT

RETIRED TEACHERS

Teachers who are retired, school administrators, nurses, nurse practitioners, midwives, counselors, and agency employees were interviewed about their professional experiences related to sexual abuse and reporting. Many of their responses are noted to discover any trends in recognizing and reporting sexual abuse.

Currently, everyone working in these professions are by law mandated reporters of abuse and sexual abuse. Let us see if we have really bridged the gap to become informed mandated reporters. The following information includes detailed responses from retired teachers regarding their experience from thirty to sixty years ago.

Many retired teachers stated that there were no official terms or recognition of sexual abuse within the school system while they were teaching. Some of the retired teachers did not comment. Some shared that no one they knew had been sexually abused. Others shared candidly of their challenges in recognizing or reporting sexual abuse.

This book preface reads: we don't know what we don't know, until we know it. A lack of information, a sense of silence, and the frustrations involved with reporting sexual abuse encapsulate the experience of these past teachers. Please acknowledge their anonymous contributions as precious. Their comments may reflect a current depiction of our local and global awareness of sexual abuse.

Next, the detailed responses from these retired teachers will be noted to provide insight as to some challenges during their time as teachers. Please consider whether any of these struggles continue today.

While working at a recently integrated school, one interviewed teacher noted that the race of the child, teacher, or principal was a factor in being told to ignore the report. Today, every Outcry, allegation, or suspected abuse is to be reported.

One teacher noted that following the law and completing an abuse report "caused me trouble with the principal." At that time, the teacher was concerned about losing their teaching job after reporting because of this interaction with the principal. Today, reports are mandatory for the teacher and administrators.

A student was transferred during the year to another teacher's class. From the information provided, this student was moved so that the student could not listen to an Outcry of sexual abuse by another student. No one spoke directly to this student. The student had no explanation of the reason for moving to another classroom with all new students. Age-appropriate sexual abuse prevention programs could have changed the outcome of this scenario.

Another teacher had the experience of being told to stop making a report because the alleged offender was predominant, important, and had power in their community. The principal told this teacher to "drop it." Mandatory means that every employee needs to report every suspected or alleged abuse and sexual abuse.

A teacher stated that a student was suicidal. The school did not want this reported due to concern about the school's insurance. Currently, the reverse would be true. Not reporting could lead to legal action with possible insurance complications.

One employee became known as the "reporter" because the number of reports by this person was considered too high. To stop the gossip, the principal prearranged to consult with this employee prior to making future reports. This system worked well in stopping the gossip.

Another teacher taught at both the university and elementary school level. In the 1980s, this teacher described that there were no terms, information, or professional continuing education related to sexual abuse. Instruction was provided in Spanish for students who spoke Spanish. This instructor stated that no one reported any abuse. During this timeframe, there was an atmosphere of silence and lack of education about sexual abuse.

Today many states are listed on the Department of Education website regarding campus-wide focus on sexual abuse prevention.

- Alaska: Trauma Engaged Schools.
- Colorado: Caring School Community. This did have a fee to use.
- Montana: VOICE, a program for prevention and support for survivors of abuses.
- Rhode Island: Great Schools.
- South Dakota and Washington: Trauma Informed.

Next, we will look at some models that may bring helpful insights for teachers, administration, and communities. One school plan and a puberty class provide information on challenges and some ideas for improvements. We will start with the basics.

CLASSROOM STATISTICS

Statistically in a classroom of thirty males, seven or eight students will report or have experienced some form of sexual abuse. For the same size classroom of females, ten students will report or have experienced some type of sexual abuse. These are estimates because they do not include the pandemic number of unspoken sexual assaults. There are several different statistics noted by different sources. To summarize, one-third or more of the students in a classroom could trust their instructor or teacher enough to make an Outcry of sexual abuse.

One agency staff member noted that the statistics have now decreased to one of ten for students under eighteen years old who will be sexually abused. This is encouraging but not acceptable.

PUBERTY CLASS

A school-based puberty program from the late 1990s establishes some tools to prevent sexual abuse. A school nurse presented the district-prepared puberty program yearly for fourth- and fifth-grade students.

Parental permission was required. Therefore, not everyone participated. The same-gender parent was always invited to attend to promote family communication about puberty. No information about boundaries or sexual abuse was included within the curriculum. Sexual abuse prevention for students needs everyone's participation.

The protocol restricted topics to those provided by a specific film developed for the district. Each student received the stipulated handout pamphlet for their gender. This technique allowed for all the material to be presented while inadvertently silencing questions and implying that many subjects were taboo. Any questions or concerns from the students other than the puberty portion of the program were not to be answered. Boundaries, sexual abuse, and abuse need to be addressed directly, with most schools now requiring age- or learning-level-appropriate curricula.

There are also matters that families feel are important to their values that need to be honored. Some states choose to address these values by deleting subjects from the curriculum. On the Utah Department of Education website, several specific topics were identified as restricted in their comprehensive health education program. These topics are premarital, extramarital, erotica, intercourse, stimulation, contraception, and erotic behavior.

This is a delicate balance of honoring family values, age-appropriate information, and student requests for facts that other students may not be ready to hear or understand. The nurse teaching the puberty class was asked about a condom seen on the floor of the local store. In staying with the protocol, this nurse shifted to hygiene and disease prevention by instructing to not touch the condom and tell the store personnel that area needed to be cleaned. Then, the next subject in the curriculum was noted. Another approach might be to briefly ask the students what they would do if they found this item on the floor, make a list, and move to the next subject. Either approach leaves the message that some things are not to be discussed.

Students may feel that they have more knowledge, whether accurate or not, about their bodies and sexual behavior. Their teachers, parents, or grandparents may have grown up in a culture of "do not talk about sex" or our private body organs defining our maleness or femaleness and their functioning. "Misinformation is epidemic," was a statement from a nurse practitioner summarizing this concern that perpetuates the cycle of sexual abuse.

If certain topics are avoided, teachers will not be able to evaluate the accuracy of the students' knowledge. Adding values can reinforce the respect of ourselves and others. Education can be provided about facts and values without restricting or avoiding topics.

During the puberty program, many of the mothers expressed that their daughters would marry and have children so there was no need for education. This concept also negates any education about sexual abuse prevention.

For the classes that were focused on English as the second language, the puberty film and handouts were in Spanish. The students and parents continued to have a discussion in their native language. Intermittently, staff was provided to translate when time allowed. The nurse who originally led the class now had no idea of what was covered or what information was shared as side comments. These side comments are often the important factor in education. They define what students know or verify what was learned or not learned. Our schools need trauma-informed bilingual employees. Funding is important for translation resources to be utilized with a scheduled program or the immediacy of an Outcry.

LANGUAGE

With a language discrepancy during an Outcry, the listener and the survivor are left with many frustrations. The listener may not comprehend that the words spoken were an Outcry. The survivor needs a compassionate Response in their indigenous language to know that they have been heard and that they were not at fault. Calling directly to Family & Protective Services, Child Protective Services, or Adult Protective Services with any concerns of an Outcry may assist in decreasing time necessary for translation.

Sexual abuse prevention programs need to be available in the different languages of the students and families or to have a translation option available. Only one department of education website—that of New York—had resources available in English and Spanish. Often an Outcry of sexual abuse would be best shared in the survivor's language of origin for accurate details and appropriate support.

Our world is coming together with COVID-19, travel, business, and some families moving to international locations. Many students and their families are living in the United States with a diverse language base from all over the world.

Currently, each educational setting needs a record of the primary language of all the students and employees. They also need to have translation options available.

With most translation services, the employee and survivor were guaranteed that everything said would be translated. Rarely, a translator was unfamiliar with a word or a dialect. This could be a valid concern for a survivor speaking about detailed aspects of the sexual abuse.

Finding a translator is time consuming and expensive. Most services charge hourly fees. One hospital utilized a portable service machine where the translator could see and be seen. Another agency phoned a service for translation. Translation services can be found on the internet. Employees were often asked to leave their job for the purpose of a time-consuming translation. Each of these options require time and money, and are best established prior to the need.

ONE SCHOOL PLAN—1990s

All school personnel were expected to work together to keep every child safe and healthy. Often in relation to abuse, employees automatically thought of counselors as being the only resource on campus.

The state of Montana included information for school counselors within their department of education under child sexual abuse prevention. The website had articles specifically for school counselors.

> For this model school, the school nurse was responsible to summarize the updated and essential information about the policies and procedures regarding abuse and sexual abuse prior to school opening every year. The nurse was trained and led groups for the Drug Free Schools program. This was a prime setting for an Outcry. Involving other staff is important in having a schoolwide plan to address sexual abuse.

In 2020, only one state, Wisconsin, had the school nurse listed with their child sexual abuse prevention information. There was a reference to the Nursing Code of Ethics with signs and symptoms of sexual abuse and information about other topics such as human trafficking.

A teacher who listens to an Outcry needs to make the original report. Teachers were often expected to use their planning time to call in the report.

> *For this school plan, the listening teacher and survivor could go to another mandated reporter who would assist with the reporting process or translation. Another option is for the teacher to call the office immediately after hearing an Outcry and request coverage in the classroom. By using some creativity, a staff member was assigned to the class in the interim. It becomes important for the interim staff to be trauma informed and prepared for this responsibility at any time. Preplanning with a known trauma team on any educational campus is essential.*

PROFESSIONAL TRAINING

All mandated reporters are required to complete an in-service or professional development program on abuse and sexual abuse. Optometrists, dentists, and other professionals are now required to complete training on human trafficking. An optometrist stated "not that I will ever have to make a report." Being prepared may save one life. Ancillary school personnel need training too.

Often the training requirements were not clear on the state department of education websites. Within the United States, the frequency ranged from every two years in Indiana and four years in Maine, as noted on the websites. Other states noted their programs of training. These included:

- California with a program on abuse and neglect.
- South Dakota listed a training guide for administration and educators on adult misconduct.
- Vermont recognized the need to train other staff: bus drivers, food services, and custodial staff members along with a guide for teachers. Only 30 percent of their staff completed this training.

- Other states listed were Kansas, Kentucky, Nebraska, Nevada, Oklahoma, Wyoming, and West Virginia.
- Missouri was the only state that noted a half-hour professional continuing credit for attending or completing online professional development programs on abuse and sexual abuse.

One possible solution for motivation could be to provide continuing education credits for teachers and all affiliated professionals for completing the required professional development related to abuse and sexual abuse. This includes the teachers, nurses, counselors, administrators, ancillary staff, dieticians, physical and occupational therapists, psychologists, vision specialists, hearing specialists, dentists, and many others.

At the beginning of the year, staff found they were engulfed with necessary information about the policies and procedures related to teaching, their school programs, and the abuse and sexual abuse information. Whether the information was presented in person or on the computer, most staff found that the abuse-related information was repetitive, overwhelming, and unnecessary, especially every year. That was until they received an Outcry. When faced with an Outcry, they remained at a loss as to what to do.

The family often protects the offenders by not reporting or recognizing an Outcry through fear, shame, or denial. Nonfamily providers establish a venue for the signs of sexual abuse and abuse to be recognized and for a survivor to make an Outcry.

Recognizing the signs of sexual abuse and making reports takes schoolwide and community involvement. Students and families need referrals to trauma-informed school staff, community resources, and medical teams.

To research and build community, the school nurse, with approval of the principal, called remote health care facilities and visited every health clinic near the school. Through this endeavor, a free clinic was established. University programs with sliding scale fees addressed dental and vision care needs. Transportation was scheduled and provided via the nurse's car (not recommended today). Hopefully, the devastating silence will be broken with additional trauma-informed health care providers involved.

Many ancillary staff noted during interviews that students were more likely to make an Outcry to a staff member who was consistent over time. A schoolwide health program developed by the nurse for all staff, parents, and students provided an informal setting for open communication. Everyone shared an open walking trail throughout the campus, vital sign monitoring, and a brief review of personal health goals. In a contest, this schoolwide design won a cash award for the school clinic. Actual participation declined throughout the year. Other means of building schoolwide and community interactions and prevention are needed.

The police and fire departments would visit the campus to establish a friendly atmosphere with students. Some students had already met these professionals in challenging situations outside of school.

Teachers would add celebrations of cultural events, such as Cinco de Mayo. There was a parade for Chinese New Year to allow children to have fun and learn. The Wisconsin school system honored April as the Sexual Assault Awareness and Child Abuse Prevention Month. The Mississippi Department of Education website has an established program called Lessons from Literature that was appropriate to use in the classroom addressing physical, verbal, and sexual abuse.

The school counselor had a referral list of resources for additional needs related to emotional health. Sharing this information assisted these professionals in working together to support students and their families in addressing difficult circumstances.

Every year, the school counselor and nurse arranged for a small health fair with various agencies providing information and resources. During the 1990s, most booths were related to medical health care, rather than resources about self-care, safety, cultural awareness, boundaries, financial, and emotional health.

Today, information about abuse and sexual abuse will be included schoolwide. A bulletin board of hotline numbers would have a place on campus, in public bathrooms, in school publications for parents and families, and in the classrooms. Prevention curricula and presentations from trauma-informed organizations would be a normal part of the schoolwide plan and the health fairs. More parents, community members, and students will be involved in the arrangements. Working together broadens our ability to find solutions. Participants are

*informed and competent in recognizing and reporting an offender
situation or an Outcry of abuse or sexual abuse.*

The one-time review of the state department of education websites
noted that there are numerous programs focused on sexual abuse prevention. The list that follows provides the results.

Safety Programs

- Ohio: Safety and Violence Prevention.
- Rhode Island and Washington: Health and Safety.
- Minnesota: Ensuring Safe and Supportive Schools.
- Idaho: Keep Idaho Safe.
- Wyoming: School Safety Summit.
- Massachusetts, Tennessee, and Texas are among other states.

Comprehensive Health Education

- Florida: Elementary Tool Kit.
- Virginia: Family Life Education.
- Massachusetts, Mississippi, Missouri, Oklahoma, and Utah.

Child Abuse Prevention

- Georgia, Hawaii, Indiana, Maryland, New Hampshire, New Jersey,
  Oklahoma, Oregon, South Dakota, Texas, Utah, Washington, Wisconsin, and Wyoming.

Statewide K–12 Sexual Abuse Curricula

- Connecticut, Indiana, Massachusetts, Pennsylvania—Key Concepts;
  Louisiana (Darkness to Light).
- The West Virginia Department of Education has developmentally
  appropriate curricula for body safety education and sexual abuse prevention. Their curriculum includes kindergarten through second
  grade in the first level; third grade through fifth in the second level;
  sixth grade through eighth grade would be the third level. The final

level spanned the ninth grade through twelfth grades. This program recognizes that developmentally appropriate information is needed to be effective in building skills for students to prevent sexual abuse.

TRAUMA-INFORMED INSTRUCTIONAL TECHNIQUES

Prior references were made to the three healing processes for the survivor that often require a response from the teacher during class. These processes are dissociation, triggers, and remembering. The emphasis here is to transform this knowledge into workable solutions that can be utilized within the classroom with trauma-informed instructional techniques.

The first healing process is *disassociation*. The survivor uses this as a shield to numb themselves during the assault. The problem is that this student continues to disassociate in the present time, which causes lack of focus. An example might be when a person nicks their finger with a paper. It takes a moment to comprehend what happened and to feel the pain. Disassociation is not helpful in the classroom or in daily life.

What a teacher may see in the classroom is a student who is staring, daydreaming, or exhibiting a glazed look. The student has lost *focus* and is not mentally present in the classroom.

The second healing process is about *triggers*. This will be a more challenging response in the classroom. Triggers appear suddenly. Others may see unrelated reactions or responses to the current environment. For the survivor, the triggers occur as an unrecognized mix of past and present. Triggers can be smells, sights, sounds, phrases, postures of others, body feelings, or anything in the current environment that reminds the survivor of the assault. The major problem for the survivor is that the trigger is real at this moment. The abuse is happening now for them in their mind and body. This becomes a matter of *safety* for the survivor.

The third healing process is *remembering*. Memories are retrieved over time. Body memories, sensations in the survivor's body or feelings, may occur. There is an aspect of putting together *puzzle pieces* of apparently unrelated stimuli with the past harm.

Let us look at each of these separately to build some trauma-informed instructional techniques.

DISASSOCIATION

Disassociation allows the person to be protected from the intensity of emotional, physical, and spiritual pain during the assault. This process is not helpful in the survivor's everyday life.

> *FOCUS. Disassociation may be demonstrated by "spacing out" or not paying attention. Students who have been sexually abused are not intentionally being inattentive. They truly are unable to focus. They have withdrawn into a space that protects while under attack. They have mixed the past and the present.*
>
> *These survivors do not recognize that they are sitting in the classroom and that they are not being hurt. Survivors need to focus and have control. As a survivor focuses, they can learn to scan their environment to remain attentive to their surroundings. Trauma-informed instructional techniques along with prevention education can help students to focus on the present.*
>
> 1. *The first exercise can begin when the teacher notices glazed-over looks from students during class. Stop the instruction. Ask students to state their first names together as a class. Each student will say their first name at the same time. This is a method of changing attention and adding focus. Ask the students as a class to name a color that they see in the classroom. This means each student states a color at the same time. This is about focus, not accuracy.*
> 2. *As the students begin to focus, an option is to offer about five to ten minutes to journal or write about what happened. Choice and control for the student is important. If they do not want to participate, they can sit and think about their favorite place, which is a meditation technique. Some will find that journaling or meditating is unfamiliar or too uncomfortable. These students may choose to do something of their choice quietly during this time.*
> 3. *When students are unfamiliar with feelings, a variety of feelings can be written on the board for information and focus. Or the teacher may ask the students to make a list of feelings and draw faces that demonstrate that feeling. Another option is to make a poster as a group project or purchase a board with faces that demonstrate different feelings. Another option is for the teacher to call out a feeling and let each student make a face that relates to*

that feeling at the same time. Any of these or variations can be focusing techniques. After a brief time, return to the lesson.

4. *Another exercise is about students learning physical body space and listening to their feelings. COVID-19 has given us some practice with this exercise by the six-foot rule of socialization. Students begin by standing in two lines facing each other with six feet in front and to each side. Ask how they are feeling. If they do not want to speak, ask them to silently note any feelings that they might have. The students will then move to the right or left to face another student. Again, noting their feelings is the next step. They usually will see that different people are associated with different feelings. This can be an exercise in focus, feelings, and body awareness. There is to be no teasing or shaming. Each students' experience is their own. There is NO right or wrong.*

Offender behaviors are demonstrated when a student is attempting to push forward when the other student has stopped. The teacher might say, "I see that STUDENT'S NAME moved forward after we stopped. Be observant. Please move back to the original stopping place."

"Physical spacings and feelings can be different for each person and will change under different circumstances. Friends usually can feel more comfortable facing each other. Facing a student who is not known as well may be extremely uncomfortable. That is wonderful. Awareness and focus are the lessons."

TRIGGERS

A person suddenly begins to cry and shouts "No one loves me." It is not clear to others what has happened. In this situation, the person was listening to a love song. This is an example of a trigger—the love song reminding the survivor of a painful experience, followed by sudden, intense reactions-crying and shouting. This survivor is reliving a hurtful experience mentally and emotionally. Feeling unloved is painful. When a bystander can recognize and state the connection, the survivor often feels understood and is able to calm.

Triggers are spurts of emotion or actions that do not appear to be related to the current situation. The survivor is mentally in a past hurtful experience. Some examples of other sudden reactions from feeling

unsafe are withdrawing, becoming restless, offensive or defensive behavior, or suddenly needing to leave. When a survivor in the classroom
reacts to a trigger, this reaction seems out of proportion and unusual to
the teacher and others present. Often the person who had the reaction
is shamed or teased which intensifies the trauma and the reaction. The
teacher and students have an opportunity to acknowledge the reaction
by providing safety and compassion as noted below in the classroom
scenario. Everyone present needs to know that they are safe in the
classroom.

This process is often difficult for the survivor because they may
realize that their actions do not match the situation. The survivor is
unable to explain, which often adds more intensity to the current situation.

> One option is for a bystander or teacher to state, "I noticed that you
> seem bothered by something. Tell me what is happening." This can
> open a dialog if appropriate in the setting. A referral may be helpful.
> SAFETY. The teacher now has the role of speaking with the survivor
> to establish that they are currently safe. State the student's name
> calmly. "This is Ms. or Mr. Teacher. This class is social studies or
> math at Trauma Elementary, Jr. High, or High School." Then suggest
> that all students take a few minutes to jot down or draw some feelings
> and thoughts on a paper or journal. The purpose is to assist all
> students in the classroom to feel safe and in control by focusing. The
> survivor may begin to realize that what they saw or felt was not
> about the present.
> As a teacher, plan settings where students can express themselves and
> their preferences. Students need to have a vote in their lives to feel
> safe.

REMEMBERING

The remembering process is a gradual one that releases small amounts
of often unrelated information over time. This innovative process is like
viewing a photo with all the details present. The person may not see all
the details at first view. Time is often needed to see the specific aspects
of a photo. This process might also be like the development of a new

lesson plan where the teacher conceptualizes some ideas or information, then develops the whole in small pieces at different times.

An adult survivor shared how she remembered more directly. She
was sitting quietly after journaling. Suddenly, she had a flash picture of
her mother orally touching her private area while she was a baby. For
this survivor, a knowing occurred. This survivor was sexually abused by
her mother as a baby.

As an adult, the survivor shared with her mother about this offending behavior. The mother's response was, "There are things we don't
talk about." The mother refused to speak any more about this assault.
The mother has currently stated that this assault never happened,
which is a form of blackout or denial.

> PUZZLE PIECES. Remembering may come as unusual, strange seg-
> ments that appear not to be connected. Be patient. Journals for stu-
> dents as assignments, whether written or sketching their thoughts,
> may help. When a student is stuck, suggest to "Tell me more as you
> think of the information." "Jot down a note about your thoughts at
> this moment." Journaling can become a normal experience in class.

FALSE MEMORY

One counselor scheduled a sexual abuse program at a known community service building. The attendance was extremely small. The night
before the program a man called the counselor, identifying himself as a
father whose daughter was saying some things about him, with no details provided. This father stated that he believed in the false memory
syndrome. The counselor listened briefly. The counselor ended the call,
noting that they had a difference of opinion.

In the experience of the author, no one can make up the trauma,
emotions, and memory process associated with any traumatic or sexual
abuse experience. Reports have been made accusing a parent or close
person of sexually abusing them. These allegations need to be evaluated
because there is some reason for the report to occur.

PREVENTION

Teaching prevention skills does not in any way imply that the student is at fault if they are sexually abused. The need to provide this type of information is indirectly making the situation the fault of the survivor. Learning prevention skills may assist a student in establishing further protection when approached or by completely avoiding a harmful situation.

TEACHABLE MOMENTS

Often there are teachable moments, a term first heard from volunteers of Planned Parenthood many years ago. These volunteers presented programs when invited for high school–level students. The purpose is not to debate this controversial aspect of parenthood. The objective is to recognize that there are moments when the information shared is inaccurate or demeaning. This is a time to provide accurate information or to add an affirming statement. If this teachable moment occurs during class, a lesson plan could be developed for a research project on the subject matter.

Often the subject of planning pregnancy brings in many factors related to spiritual or personal practices that were found to be offensive and unnatural by some. For example, a program for parents only was offered after school. During the program, condoms were offered to only those parents who wanted them at no charge. This was offensive to many parents, who reported this to the principal. The principal chose to close the presentation.

One perspective regarding this example was that continuing the program against the wishes of the majority would have been offensive. Conversely, is it detrimental for some to not receive education related to all choices? A compromise is that those parents wanting additional information and supplies could contact the agency directly. This dichotomy is a continuing dilemma within our school systems related to the subject of sexual abuse prevention and education.

OPEN OR CLOSED COMMUNICATION

Many adults need education, counseling, or spiritual support in learning about safety and boundaries related to their bodies, spirit, and minds. A ninety-year-old elder once shared with their adult child that the partner usually wanted sex more than they did. The elder was not able to say no; the partner went ahead with sex, apparently not aware or not caring about the other person's need to stop.

The adult child went into lecture mode, which does not work well to open communication. The adult child explained that the elder had the right to say "no." The partner needs to stop when the other person does not respond. The adult child went on to explain that if the partner continued to push for sex after a no or silence, then this was considered sexual abuse. With all this great information, the parent stopped talking with the adult child, that is, closed communication.

The adult child in this situation had suspected sexual and physical abuse as a possibility in the parents' relationship in the past. When asked directly, the adult child always received a denial of abuse from their parent. Was this a case that needed reporting? One can call and review this scenario with the agency accepting reports.

> To open communication for an adult student and their teacher, the teacher can mirror, which means to repeat what the student said— "Your partner wants sex more than you"—for the purpose of having a conversation. "What are some ways that you can tell your partner that you do not want to have sex as often?" Whatever the subject, mirroring or repeating what was said in a nonjudgmental tone often opens communication.

PROTECTING STUDENTS

Many students want accurate information without knowing how to ask. Others may think that they will not receive an answer regarding their questions linked to safety and boundaries. Since these questions are often related to private areas of the body and the differences in how families approach these concerns, the student has understood indirectly that they are not to ask or often has been denied the information requested, whether at home or at school.

One teacher found herself on a teen chat line while at home. This teacher recognized that the teens were giving each other inaccurate information that could lead to teen pregnancy and the transmission of life-threatening diseases, such as HIV and hepatitis.

At first, this teacher identified as an adult and shared a lot of accurate information with these teens. After a short time, this teacher recognized that she would not be able to clear up all the misinformation and withdrew from the chat line. This is not a workable solution to this problem.

Another note of concern is the fact that an adult was on a teen chat line. A teen chat line with teens talking about sexual matters would be perfect for an offender to begin building a bond. By sharing that he or she was of a similar age and sympathizing with their problems, the offender has begun to groom these teens for various types of sexual abuse. During the grooming, the offender's purpose would be to meet with one or more of these teens, thus isolating them from the group.

This thought of an offender on a teen chat line might come to most people's minds if the teacher was a male. Females can also be offenders. There has been an increase in women educators who are alleged or suspected of sexually abusing their students. Students need information or a plan to answer questions that may arise.

DEPARTMENT OF EDUCATION

Conversely, our state department of education websites are addressing the lack of response for student questions. With expertise in establishing developmentally appropriate curricula for the different cognitive levels of various students, our state websites list various programs that are currently being used to address the concerns of our students related to health, safety, and boundaries. Some websites had a multitude of information for students, families, staff, volunteers, and the community, while other websites did not list clear material. The details of this informal survey are summarized in chapter 3. The development of tools and resources for all ages is necessary to decrease and hopefully end this perpetuating cycle of sexual abuse.

For educators, families, and staff, protecting our students is of extreme importance. Many survivors within a noted support group felt that not having information about saying no and what sexual abuse prevention involves was sexual abuse. Some might not agree with labeling a lack of skills, training, and information as sexual abuse.

A child or youth is vulnerable when they have not been given enough information to learn how to say no at an age-appropriate level or to avoid risky situations. The Utah Department of Education has a sexual abuse curriculum that includes refusal skills. Older students also need information about how to make choices about participating in the wide range of sexual behavior. Not having the skills, education, and protection can be devastating.

SUMMARY

From retired teachers to mandated reporters, our educational system has progressed in acknowledging and supporting survivors of sexual abuse. With additional emphasis on viewing clues of sexual abuse as trauma responses rather than disruptive behavior, teachers have the option to utilize trauma-informed techniques in the classroom.

Chapter 3 discusses concerns and suggestions for future utilization by educators and within our educational systems to promote compassion and campus-wide prevention of sexual abuse. Additional agency, prison, faith-based, and addiction-based programs also provide information regarding sexual abuse for students of all ages, families, neighbors, and communities.

3

FUTURE RESPONSES

ME TOO

The MeToo Movement originally began on social media in 2006 by Tarana Burke, who is a sexual harassment survivor and activist.[1] This movement provides empathy for those who have been sexually harassed or sexually abused and education for the public about sexual violence. The MeToo Movement influenced the making of Mulan, the movie. Mulan originally was to have a love relationship with the commander character. Through education from the MeToo Movement, it was recognized that having a relationship with a supervisor would be sexual harassment or sexual abuse. When the movie was produced, Mulan developed a friendship with an equally ranked person that later became a respectful, love relationship.

COVID-19

To remain healthy, we all need boundaries to maintain safety and well-being. With COVID-19, the importance of boundaries has been magnified. Social distancing by staying six feet away from another person and wearing a mask over the nose and mouth are the two primary boundaries. People need to be educated and reminded of six-foot spacing and how to wear masks. Learning, reviewing, and honoring boundaries are concepts that are necessary for healing from sexual abuse.

Children of all ages have been home with their parents all day. Many parents and other adults are working, attending classes, or both on computers from home. Students of any age and their families will be spending more time together, which can increase stress tremendously or present the possibility of more quality time together. Again, people need education and guidance in coping with stress in a healthy manner and how to establish quality time with loved ones.

Many sources have offered education, assistance, and information on how to take care of ourselves physically and emotionally during this time. One program was aired early in the pandemic on Houston's KHOU Channel 11 on April 3, 2020 at 7:00 p.m. central time. This COVID-19 special presented assistance in accurately answering questions about financial matters, entrepreneurial businesses, parenting tips, socializing, physical health, and especially about emotional health related to this new disease.

Sexual abuse is about broken trust and broken boundaries. Sadly, this same program noted that there has been a 35% increase in domestic violence, which often includes sexual abuse within Montgomery county in Texas.[2] Sexual abuse and all types of abuse thrive on isolation.

School has reopened virtually and in person with six-foot spacing and masks. This new situation will add additional stress for educators and students. One teacher shared that her school district had an all-day professional development program on trauma-informed practices about how to calm oneself and be observant to the signs and symptoms of abuse and sexual abuse.

Offenders do not and will not honor boundaries. Isolation is their offense breeding ground. Sexual abuse has increased during this time of isolation and fear. With our families and students on the internet more often, there will be more exposure to online offenders. Many people may overuse or abuse drugs, alcohol, sex, and violence to cope, thus adding to the number of offenders and the severity of violence.

Some communities are listing the 24/7 hotline numbers for sexual assault and domestic violence support and assistance. Violence has increased within our communities during this time of crisis. Resources need to be increased as well.

Educators must be mindful of any changes in a student's behavior, comments, and ability to focus of their studies as they interact virtually or in person. This is especially important during a disaster, family emergency or change, or world crisis, such as COVID-19. These behaviors can indicate possible abuse or sexual abuse.

Our communities have actively come together to find solutions. We are developing a new way of living with this worldwide threat to health. Most crises bring people together to share kindness and compassion while establishing workable solutions. Hopefully, we can transfer this cooperation to explore and discover effective ways to prevent sexual abuse.

The next section will provide definitions and trauma-informed responses for a variety of types of sexual abuse. For many of us, these well-thought-out scenarios provide a new approach that will require learning, reviewing, and practice for a personal compassionate response.

DEFINING TYPES OF SEXUAL ABUSE

All sexual abuse includes a devastating invasion, without acknowledged consent, of a survivor's personal body space, sexual organs, and emotional, spiritual, and physical well-being. During sexual abuse or any abuse, a distinct spiritual loss occurs with the intense feelings of hopelessness and helplessness felt by the survivor. These scenarios will be difficult to read when one truly recognizes the extent of the cruel treatment.

> *Within the descriptions that follow of various types of sexual abuse, areas will continue to be utilized to indicate school or educationally based settings and scenarios with trauma-informed responses and summaries. Here are some definitions developed from blending survivor experiences.*

Sexual Violence, Sexual Assault

This includes all types of sexual abuse; forced sexual behavior; being attacked in a sexual manner with no choice by a known or unknown offender.

Sexual assault or sexual violence is not just the violent act of intercourse. Touching any area of the body including the sexual organs without permission is violence. The offender often grooms or indoctrinates a survivor over time to obtain power and control. With sexual abuse, there can be covert or overt threats to the survivor or someone close to the survivor of sexual, physical, financial, emotional, spiritual, or social harm or death. Gifts and praise furnish an illusion of friendship or romance during the attack. Offenders ignore the reality that silence or no answer or no response means "no!"

Florida, Nevada, North Dakota, and Ohio have a sexual assault program listed on their websites under the Department of Education. Some states have specific curriculum which are listed here.

- Louisiana: Darkness to Light Sexual Abuse Prevention
- Mississippi: Love is Abuse Curriculum
- New Mexico: SSAS—Stop Sexual Assault in Schools
- Pennsylvania: SESAME—Stop Educator Sexual Abuse, Misconduct, and Exploitation

Campuswide Scenario

Education about Sexual Abuse

The drama department is presenting a play which involves sexual abuse, gaslighting, use of power for sexual favor, domestic violence, grooming, and other forms of abuse. Currently, this event will need to be coordinated in a manner that provides social distancing, masks, and COVID precautions.

A trauma informed approach will encourage campus-wide participation. The music department could record related music for the opening or intermission. The art department can provide classes devoted to creating or researching related art to be displayed. Parents and families can present information about this topic. Community and school organizations will want to be available to provide information and resources on the topic. Other campus related departments need to be involved such as security, maintaince, dietary staff, school nurses, counselors, ancillary personnel, and other programs on campus.

Each class whether children or adult students will chose an age appropriate topic related to sexual abuse prevention or resources. Boundaries about depicting details, graphic images, and cussing will definitely limit expression. These will also provide safety for persons who have experienced sexual abuse and maybe triggered.

Individuals or groups will research and present the data. The focus is on presenting solutions and prevention ideas. Topics related to sexual abuse could be:

- *refusal skills*
- *what to do when someone calls another a name*
- *how to say no*
- *how abuse/trauma effects us*
- *how to report and who to call*
- *how to support a friend who has been sexually abused*
- *what to say*
- *topic of compassion*
- *where to get help in school*
- *how to get help in your neighborhood*
- *safety at school*
- *safety while walking to school*
- *community organizations that provide resources*
- *school organizations that help*
- *recess-respectful play*
- *internet safety*
- *what to do if you see someone getting hurt*
- *what characteristics are important in someone you date*
- *how to make friends.*

All of these submissions can be emailed to a coordinator that can print and place them throughout the campus, thus respecting COVID precautions. Any of these topics can be used as a topic for classroom instruction in the future.

Groping

Groping is touching near or on a sexual organ or part of the body—an offender grabbing or touching sexual parts of another person's body without permission. This behavior usually provides the illusion of power and possible sexual pleasure for the offender.

An example could be a pat on the buttock or being brushed against on purpose to feel sexual parts of the body. "Cop a feel" is one slang term for this sexual abuse behavior.

A true example of groping was a woman being touched near her breasts by a man walking the other direction in the corridors of her apartment complex. Her response was "Well excuse you!"

The survivor was shocked, felt invaded, and believed that she was unsafe for months after the assault. She was uncertain about calling the police because law enforcement might think the sexual abuse was minor. The main impression that she had related to the man's identity was that he seemed normal, like any other man. Normal was not enough information to make a report in her opinion. Shame and not knowing what to do often causes survivors to remain voiceless.

This sexual abuse was reported to the apartment manager who was aware of this man sexually abusing women by groping. The offender was eventually arrested. A more helpful solution would have been to report this sexual abuse at the time to the police with any data that the survivor could remember.

> *School scenario—groping. A teacher observes a student walking in a different direction reach out and grab at the genital area of another student's jeans.*
>
> *Response: "Let's talk about what I just saw happen," in a calm voice. "Tell me please. I want to understand." Listen. Then summarize the situation by commenting: "I saw a student grabbing at the genital area (or private area if younger students) of another student's jeans. This is not OK. What are you going to do differently?"*
>
> *Groping behavior is sexual abuse and may indicate that either student is a survivor of sexual abuse. Discussing this event with the trauma team on campus, principal, nurse, or counselor is an option. Calling in a report to the appropriate agency personnel for guidance on reporting or making a referral is another option. Discussing this occurrence with the parents if the student is underage is important and may need coordination with a referral to a counselor on campus to provide education for the parents.*

Fondling

Fondling is sexual touching with continued movements or stimulation. A survivor's body might naturally react in a sexual manner. This does not in any way indicate that this assault was welcomed.

One survivor shared that she was fondled by a man who stood behind her on an elevator at work. This man reached from the back and felt of her breasts. Then he asked, "Did that make you feel uncomfortable?" When she said, "Yes," he smiled and said "Good!"

The survivor reported this sexual abuse to her supervisor, who believed this report. This offender was a member of the management's family and was a community pastor. When confronted, he admitted to the behavior.

The offender apologized as ordered directly to the survivor. This forced apology was not believed by the survivor. Being near this offender was extremely uncomfortable for the survivor. In conclusion, the offender was not to interact with this woman in any way. The survivor actively avoided this offender during her employment out of fear for herself and her child for a long while after the assault. This sexual abuse happened in the 1970s and was not reported to the authorities.

> *School scenario—fondling. Two students are under the slide to the side of the playground at recess undressed below the waist touching each other in sexual areas. A teacher sees them.*
>
> *Response: "Please put on your clothes and let us talk. I will wait for you over here. Tell me what you were doing." Listen, then summarize. "I saw one student who is undressed being touched on the genitals or private areas by the other child who is also undressed. This is not OK. What other things can you do during recess?"*
>
> *These behaviors can be a sign of sexual abuse. As more details are noted, this could be exploration or sexual violence by a young offender repeating what was taught from being sexually abused. Again, calling the official agency can provide clarity about the need to report. Include all the interaction with your responses while on the call. Both set of parents also must be notified.*
>
> *If this occurs with young adults, education and more information is needed to evaluate this situation.*

Sexual Harassment

Sexual harassment involves any unwanted sexually oriented attention, unwanted touch, or sexual conversations. This includes sexually implied or themed jokes. Harassment occurs when someone attempts to discuss sexual matters or make a suggestive comment toward a sexual behavior when in a nonsexual setting, workplace, or event.

Sexual harassment can be required or requested sexual behavior from someone in power. It can occur from a person in authority— supervisor, boss, or administrator. An example, whether stated or implied, is "To keep this job, you will touch me in a sexual manner or have sex with me."

The survivor is often legally expected to document the first refusal related to this sexual abuse before an official report can be made. Again, the survivor is left responsible to report and stop this unwanted sexual behavior.

Five states—Illinois, Iowa, Kentucky, South Dakota, and Virginia— have sexual harassment information listed on their department of education websites under child sexual abuse prevention.

> School scenario—sexual harassment. One teacher continues to tell sexually or racially oriented jokes. Most people standing nearby ignore the joke or laugh. Another teacher states, "That joke is offensive to me. Please stop. Thank you." This interaction needs to be written and submitted to the appropriate person as noted in the campus or district policies and procedures. On the next break, this joke teller continues with more jokes. "Please stop. These jokes are offensive to me. Please stop telling them." Others may say "It's just a joke." "No." The survivor writes another report listing who was present, with another request to stop the sexually or racially oriented jokes.

Sexual or Gender Discrimination

Members of a certain gender are targeted, put under duress or physically harmed because of their choice of expression regarding personal masculinity or femininity. Gender discrimination involves being teased, harassed, or bullied about one's gender or sexual orientation.

Although it is now illegal, many people continue to be harassed about their sexual orientation or gender. Only two state departments of education, those of Montana and New Hampshire, had specific information listed about the lesbian, gay, bisexual, transgender, and queer (LGBTQ) sexual orientation.

School scenario—gender or sexual discrimination—beauty school campus. At a beautician training program, the students are gossiping about a male teacher. The assumption was made that this man was gay because he chose to be a beauty school instructor as a career. One's gender or sexual orientation has no bearing on a person's professional performance or choice of career. Harassment is now illegal. One trauma-informed solution was for this instructor to speak with his supervisor. The supervisor and instructor decided to add a class on discrimination for the students. Consequences for continuing the harassing gossip were noted. A zero-tolerance policy was implemented where each student would be given one opportunity to end this behavior. After that time, their harassing behavior would be reported to law enforcement, and they would be withdrawn from the program. Providing education is an important beginning in changing our perspective.

Commercially Sexually Exploited Children, Youth, or Adults

This involves child, youth, or adult trafficking; child or youth prostitution; sex slaves; selling or abducting children, youth, or adults for sex or pornography; groups of people using children, youth, or adults to have sex. It also includes paying for sex with someone under the legal age of adulthood per state law and being groomed into service with gradual pressure to shift the responsibility to the survivor.

School scenario—commercial sexual exploitation. A teacher hears another teacher bragging about going to a prostitute frequently. The nickname and a brief description of the prostitute was stated. One of the students in your eighth-grade class often goes by that name and appears to be remarkably like the description. This student has been dozing in class and is not completing assignments. This student often acts in a sexually enticingly manner around other students. As a trauma-informed teacher, you become concerned that your student may be a survivor of sexual abuse through prostitution and grooming.
Response: To the student, "I am concerned about the behaviors that I see in the classroom, such as dozing and not completing assignments. I have noticed you speaking frequently about sexual matters with other students. I am concerned. I want to hear how your life is going right now." Listen because the student may feel more comfortable to

share with you. "I feel that help is needed and am making a referral to the counselor to explore some options for assistance. Please feel free to speak with me too." This teacher needs to make a report to Family & Protective Services and the police.

Response: The bragging teacher: Report what you heard this teacher say on the referral to the counselor and to Family & Protective Services. Work as a team to protect the student. Follow-up with the bragging teacher will be needed in another conversation.

Human Trafficking

Human trafficking has the characteristic of exchanging something of value for sex with a survivor who is groomed into this service. Value may be defined by the child, youth, or adult survivor who has nothing and is looking for family or friends. A valuable exchange for sex could be a place to stay, rent, drugs, alcohol, money, food, clothes, a cheap piece of jewelry, or any material item deemed of value.

The common thread is that most survivors continue to feel they made the decision to participate. This bonds the survivor to the trafficker who used grooming to engage and set this mindset. This false sense of "making the decision" to participate often continues until the survivor later gets help in most cases.

Most frequently, this sexual abuse begins with children, youth, or adults seeking friends or relationships on the internet. The survivor believes what the internet offender tells them. The internet offender e-mails that they are of a similar age and have similar problems with friends, family, school, or relationships to build a connection. The child, youth, or adult is left with the thought and feeling that they made this decision to become friends or romantic partners. Later, the survivors are expected to have sex with whoever, whenever, and how often the trafficker decides while continuing to think this was their idea.

The survivors of human trafficking are generally found through reports of sexual abuse or being arrested by the police. Survivors are often considered criminals rather than victims of sexual abuse. Survivors continue to feel that this situation was their choice, thus adding to the denial of being sexually abused. The impact of the sexual abuse for the survivor comes later if at all for these survivors.

Colorado is the only state having an internet safety program listed on the department of education websites. They include restrictions for the use of library computers on campus. Texas has information about cyber bullying within one of their curricula. Many states utilize the computer for sexual abuse training and education for employees, parents, and students. Most computers have been designed to have blocks on certain websites for use in school or at home.

Florida was the first state to develop a program related to human trafficking, in 2019. Several state programs are now available through the department of education in South Carolina, South Dakota, Texas, Virginia, Washington, and Wisconsin. Ohio has a teen trafficking program for parents and educators.

School scenario—human trafficking. A teacher notices that a young student has a lot of money in hand. When asked, this student shows the teacher an e-mail from a new friend who has sent the money by another student at school. As a teacher who has learned about human trafficking, you are concerned. This was the first e-mail to the student from two days ago. The student had provided the requested information, which was the numbers and the name of the bank that the parents frequently used. This student was so proud to have remembered the numbers to the account to help these two new friends share the money. This student did not understand that the cash is from the parents' account. Nor did the student understand that this is an extremely dangerous situation that can include sexual abuse.

Response: After a moment (or more) of shock, the teacher states, "Sending you money was a nice gesture. I am concerned about your new friends wanting to share their money. Let us go tell your story to the vice principal. You are not in trouble."

A staff member was assigned to the classroom while this teacher called in a report to CPS and 911. Child Protectives Services and police requested that the parents be called after their interviews with the students involved.

Often the classroom students know the assigned classroom staff member and will ask "What's happening to NAME of STUDENT?" or start gossiping about what they have seen or heard in the neighborhood. Technically, the staff member would not know the details due to confidentiality. The safety of the student is at stake. While in the classroom, this trauma-informed staff member will be listening to the comments of the students who are sharing. Any additional informa-

tion, no matter how unrelated it may seem, can be added in another report by using the case number provided by Family & Protective Services. These details may be a vital link.

One tool noted in this scenario is having a campus-wide trauma team of mandated reporters available for school staff and student support during an Outcry. The team can assign assistance in the classroom and be available while the teacher makes the report.

Another tool is confidentiality, which is vital for student and staff safety to link the persons involved. The third tool is the trauma-informed foundation for all employees to be aware of potentially dangerous situations. One school district provided an all-day professional development seminar about trauma-informed techniques prior to school starting in 2020.

The fourth is to be alert and listen to any side comments. No matter how unrelated these communications may seem, they need to be shared with the team member and added to the report by using the case number assigned by Family & Protective Services. A fifth tool is to provide age-appropriate education regarding personal safety.

Post report: The parents and student were given appointments to a family therapist through Family & Protective Services to provide trauma-informed therapy for the whole family.

Sextortion

Sextortion involves threats to a person's safety or the betrayal of exposing sensitive or private material that the survivor had provided through the internet. This personal material can be held as a threat to the survivor. Requests made by the offender range from demanding that the survivor send sexual images of themselves, provide sexual favors, or pay money. This happens online from offenders portraying themselves as friends or lovers. The survivor becomes a perpetrator with an illusion of no further harm to themselves. The author found the term in an FBI video while researching the District of Columbia website.[3]

University scenario—sextortion. One trauma-informed professor teaching at the university level realized that sextortion was an unfamiliar term. The university class took a vote and agreed unanimously to see the above-noted video because no one in the class had heard this term. During the discussion many of the students expressed concern for their children, grandchildren, and great-grandchildren. The professor listened and heard the adult student concerns. The professor planned an assignment for the students to develop role plays for having family discussions about sextortion for older children, computer safety for younger children, and my body is mine conversation for younger children and children with special comprehension needs. The assignment required documented research on age-appropriate content related to children with different levels of comprehension.

Response: student with their family—"We saw a video today in class about something called sextortion or personal safety while using the computer [if younger] or someone trying to hurt my body [very young]. Tell me something that you know about this subject. Let us talk about sextortion or safety." These replies can be modified for individuals with learning challenges.

Rape

Rape is forced sexual approach, touch, or intercourse. Often, the survivor knows the offender. Some common names for rape are gang rape, gang bang, marital rape, marriage rape, date rape, teen dating violence, drugged rape, intoxicated rape, sibling-to-sibling rape, and child-to-child rape. The author added and named another one, disease rape. All of these can include physical, emotional, financial, spiritual, and verbal abuse combined with sexual abuse.

Lifelong learning scenario—rape. A student in the lifelong learning program approached the instructor after class and began to share about a date last weekend. This elder adult student shared about being confused and wanting to say no to sex but felt scared and could not speak. She had not been on any dates since her husband died several years ago. The offender had stated that they have a date for Saturday at 7:00 p.m.

Response: "I hear that you were afraid and felt that you did not have a choice. You are not at fault. Let us call Adult Protective Services together since this person is still in your life."

When making a report, the 4Ws are noted: who, what, when, and where. The instructor guided this survivor in providing the information over the phone. The teacher can offer to sit with this adult student while the date is canceled. A teacher might suggest the student write about alternative solutions in meeting people, such as meeting in a public place with your own transportation or programs for groups while getting to know new people. Again, this topic might make a great lesson plan for youth or adult students.

Marital or marriage rape is when a person is not asked or not given the chance to say no to sexual behavior, even in a committed marriage. Marriage does not give anyone permission to be sexual at any time or any place. Both persons must agree to sexual activity.

Date rape or teen dating violence. While on a date, an offender does not stop sexual behavior or conversation when asked. Or the offender continues because no answer was provided, which meant "yes" to the offender. When the survivor is silent, silence means "no." To proceed is rape. Teen dating violence includes other forms of abuse and violence in conjunction to the sexual abuse.

Drug rape is being given alcohol or drugs to force or accomplish rape or other sexual abuse without permission. A person so intoxicated or drugged that they have lost the ability to stop or refuse, or an intoxicated person forcing another to be sexual physically or conversationally is drug rape.

Disease rape is a term the author developed for offenders who have sexual intercourse for the sole purpose of transmitting COVID-19 or a sexually transmitted disease, such as HIV or hepatitis. The underlying motivational factors for the offender could be feelings of anger, rage, or resentment. The circumstances may be assault or grooming for the illusion of a relationship.

This betrayal is deep. The survivor will need education about the sexually transmitted diseases. Testing may occur immediately and require a repeat later to ensure accuracy. Counseling can be helpful while waiting for the second test results as well as addressing the betrayal.

Incarcerated rape. A prisoner charged and imprisoned for sexual abuse offenses often has been sexually abused as a child. This trauma needs to be addressed directly with trauma-informed staff for change to occur. One person who visits the prisons for ministry described a large, in-your-face, offensive type of guy crying while sharing about the sexual abuse that he had endured as a child. Some offenders may be willing to start on this courageous journey while many will become more skilled at offending.

Unfortunately, this prisoner survivor is likely to be sexually abused by prison guards or other prisoners. No matter what anyone's opinion is about sentencing and incarceration, sexual abuse creates sexual abusers as referenced in sibling-to-sibling rape and child-to-child rape. Survivors became offenders, who in turn become survivors in a repetitious cycle of sexual abuse.

One survivor spoke of being sexually abused by both parents. She continued to make self-damaging choices in her life. As a child, she had sexually touched her brother and other children in the family and neighborhood. With trauma-informed counseling and a support system of other survivors, she stopped communication with her offending parents out of fear and concern about wanting to hurt them in retaliation. This survivor faced her offender thoughts and behaviors, both present and past.

She was able to find some compassion for her offending parents as she found some peace in recognizing that each of us has an offender and survivor inside. Both of her parents had been sexually abused themselves and then repeated the cycle by sexually abusing her. All sexual abuse and abuses need to stop.

Grooming

Grooming is a process where an offender uses statements of blame, aggression, threatening words or gestures, or violent acts to gain power over a survivor.

One recovering offender shared his journey of getting help. The offender describes the mental state while offending as getting into a "zone." There were noted skills of manipulating and cultivating. This person stated with sadness that these skills could have been used in more positive ways. "This is a bad example to learn from. What was I thinking? I was not." That is the point. Offenders are driven to avoid their feelings at all cost through violence.

To stop the sexual abuse cycle, this person has continued working for years on himself by attending support groups, a treatment center for sexual addiction, and counseling with a certified sex addiction therapist.[4]

This offender is married. Both spouses are in programs to support their growth and recovery. Together, they set a specific time weekly to share how each is doing. This offender does not recognize any sexual abuse at the time of this writing. "Offenders need something to snap them [offenders] out of this unconscious drive or bubble." For an of-fender, this snap could be bystander mobilization and the report of an Outcry.

Seduction

This concept of enticing someone to have sex or to be romantically involved is a myth that perpetuates sexual abuse. Each person has choice.

Hazing

Hazing is considered an initiation into a group, such as sororities, frater-nities, bands, athletics, and military. To join, one must do a set of demeaning, physically challenging, and emotionally degrading activities that are physically, emotionally, sexually, and spiritually abusive. People have lost their lives from hazing. The use or overuse of alcohol and/or drugs has also been noted as the cause of death. Consent comes from peer pressure and is not considered true legal consent.[5]

> High school scenario—hazing. A student in class is dozing and not paying attention. Another student notices and makes a loud noise to get the first student's attention. The student responds by screaming and placing their hands over their head, which is shocking to all. This trauma-informed teacher understands that the scream and protective movement are reactive, and a sign of trauma endured. The teacher provides an assignment for the class to write about their response to focus the class and have time to talk with this student. The student shares about being an official member of the band now. Having been trauma informed and aware that the band had no functions sched-uled the night before, the teacher listens to the Outcry. The teacher walks with this student to the nurse, who is part of the trauma team. The nurse calls for a staff member to go to the classroom as prear-ranged, to remain until the teacher can return after making the origi-nal Outcry report. While using the same assigned case number, the school nurse will call in an additional report to the report agency regarding the Outcry. The nurse will only screen for life-threatening care—breathing, bleeding. Performing any other care may remove evidence. A call to 911 can be made if injuries need immediate atten-

tion. The parents will be called as Child Protective Services or 911 recommends.

Gaslighting

Gaslighting consists of the offender defending their offensive behavior, discounting the survivor's perceptions, and can include domestic violence. Gaslighting is any spoken words, gestures, or influences that have the result of the survivor questioning themselves or their perceptions.[6]

Stalking

Stalking consists of an offender repeatedly following a chosen survivor. This sexual abuse is often intimidating and feels threatening to the survivor. The offender may feel sexual pleasure from the act of stalking.

Sexual Bullying

Sexual bullying is using name calling, cruel, malicious, vindictive comments about another person's body, gender, or sexual orientation, and by adding physical violence.

Thirteen states have listings for antibullying programs on their department of education websites under child sexual abuse prevention. These states are Georgia, Hawaii, Illinois, Iowa, Kentucky, Maine, Minnesota, Nebraska, New Mexico, North Dakota, Oklahoma, South Dakota, and Texas.

> *School scenario—elementary—transgender. A trauma-informed teacher hears students calling out "Tranny, MTF, FTM" while taunting a first grader. For a moment, nothing registers for the teacher. These students are bullying this student. More definition occurs as the teacher thinks about sexual abuse continuing education programs and connects the information. The student, at six years old, wants to change genders.*
>
> *The teacher becomes involved as a bystander and speaks to the taunting students. "These mean comments need to stop. This is bullying. Please do so now. These mean comments hurt. Do not repeat this bullying. Thank you."*

This teacher speaks briefly with the first grader. "If someone starts saying mean things again, ask them to stop, and tell others around you that the words hurt." Listen. "I am hearing initials that normally go with someone changing genders. Tell me about yourself." Listen. "Thank you for sharing with me. Our school has a gay alliance with counselors and the Montrose Center has programs called Hatch and Hatchlings for people eight to twenty-one years old. I will write down the information."

MTF means transgender from male to female. This female will be addressed as a female, her, she. FTM means transgender from female to male. This male will be addressed as he, him. [7]

Voyeurism

Voyeurism is looking at people without their knowledge or permission while they dress, undress, are unclothed, or being sexual with another person. "Peeping Tom" is a common term for voyeurism.

School scenario—third grade—voyeur. In a physical education class, one of the students continually changed quickly and watched others shower and change. The trauma-informed teacher was told by other students and sat with the student for a few minutes after class in the main gym area. "I understand that you are watching others taking a shower. Tell me about this."

This student wanted information about how their sexual organs and body worked. This young male student wanted to know about the action of the penis called erection. The female student wanted to know if blood from a period goes on the floor during a shower.

Teacher: "Thank you for asking me. Watching others while they shower is not the best idea. This is to be private time. What you asked is a normal body function. Is there someone that you trust to ask when you have other questions? Or maybe a library book about the growing body might help."

Can the teacher answer these questions directly? What do the policies and procedures state? Go with brief true answers. "Yes, some blood from a period can go to the floor during a shower. The body is made that way. If you notice a lot of blood, please let me know. Thank you for being concerned and asking what you wanted to know." "Your penis is made to be in both positions as you grow older.

The body is made that way. Thank you for asking about what you wanted to know."
Many teachers have been presented with similar situations. Deciding what to say can be challenging. Short, brief answers are best. Take time to respond. Often, the students are learning and want only the basics.

Exhibitionism

Exhibitionism is showing others who have not given their permission one's sexual organs or genitals. "Exposing themselves" is a common term—showing one's sexual body parts or touching themselves or masturbating in public.

> *School scenario—junior high—exhibitionism. A teacher notices a student touching themself sexually or masturbating in the corner while on the school campus. The teacher needs to stand where they can be seen by others. "I am uncomfortable with you touching yourself sexually in public. Please stop."*
> *Student. "Others enjoy seeing me do this. What's with you, Teach?"*
> *Teacher comments in a calm voice because the student's sexual behavior has nothing to do with the teacher. If there is a crowd, the teacher can use bystander mobilization and state, "This student touching themself in public is against the law (or is not OK or needs to be done in private). Please get back to your class or studies."*
> *Disrespect does need to be addressed as well as the sexual behavior. "Saying mean things will not erase your public sexual behavior. We will go to the counselor (vice principal, or other trauma-informed person) to discuss help for you to stop."*

Sexual Racial Violence

Sexual racial violence is using people for sex or making sexual threats only because they are of another race. Prejudices were noted within their own race due to the variation of their skin tones or color.

One retired teacher had wondered while growing up why the neighbor children of one black woman were of various shades of color from light white tones to dark black tones. As an adult, the teacher learned that this mother of thirteen children had been sexually abused by several white slave masters throughout her life. This black woman was sexually abused for no other reason than her race and the norms of society. The conversation did not describe how this family was treated by others. Neither this survivor woman nor her children are at fault for this sexual abuse.

> *School scenario—racial violence. An adult white survivor shared the experience of being forced as a child to participate in torturing and killing of black people. This racial violence had been perpetrated intergenerationally for years. This child survivor was praised for being able to use a knife skillfully. Sexual abuse by family and community was a constant for this child. This child survivor was forced to terminate pregnancies caused by the sexual abuse while being praised for ending the life of these babies.*
> *This description only alludes to the depth of torment felt by a child who senses that something is not right, is praised for being an offender, and lives with fear every single day. This torment decreases with trauma-informed help and self-compassion while healing from childhood violence and sexual abuse.*

Sexting

Sexting is using the phone to text about sexual matters, send sexually explicit pictures, or to solicit sexual partners. This practice is shared by people who are in relationships to enhance their romantic life. This is dangerous for children, teens, young adults, and adults seeking instant friendships and relationships. Sexting if misused is a felony.

> *School-based scenario—sexting. As a trauma-informed instructor in a lifelong learning program, you are adding a course related to senior adult sexuality titled "What you need to know about violence, not sex." As an instructor creating your lesson plan, you watch OK, Inc.'s video* Sexting: A Documentary *on YouTube. This provides accurate information and workable ideas to inform students of all ages and their families about the dangers of sexting.* [8]

Forced Marriage

Forced marriage is common in some cultures. Another term might be an arranged marriage with the dynamic of having no choice or an illusion of choice for either person. In some states, parents are legally able to give consent for the marriage of an underaged child.[9]

Conjugal Slavery or Forced Conjugal Association

These are other terms for forced marriage because marriage still implies consent.[10]

Child or Youth Marriage

This is the marriage of a child or youth under eighteen years old. If an underage person is pregnant, in some states she can legally make choices and consent as an adult.

> *School scenario—child marriage. One contemporary teacher shared that a young female student in the classroom was from another country where this student was considered an adult. Culturally, this "child" can be married, with consummation and the hope of soon having children expected at the age of nine, while in Western culture, this is considered sexual abuse.*

Sexual Misconduct

Sexual misconduct is utilized for an offender of sexual abuse within the school system. This behavior may include any sexual behaviors that would be alarming or affronting to another, exhibitionism, rape, or sexual behavior in front of a third party without consent.[11]

Domestic Violence

Domestic means in a committed relationship. Violence is when a spouse has no choice about being sexual or in what way to be sexual within a marriage. This usually co-occurs with other types of abuses.

> *College-based scenario—an offender's thought process related to domestic violence and sexual assault. This offender had been reported and counseled twice for yelling and making insulting remarks to his*

boss and coworkers. He has continued with this offensive behavior and is told on payday that he is fired. Offender thinking and actions follow.

His boss does not understand and cannot handle him expressing himself. He needs to get a job with a better boss and more money anyway. At home, he demands that his wife go to purchase beer for him while verbally abusing her and hitting her because she does not have beer in the refrigerator already. Suddenly, he is accusing his spouse of not loving him the way he deserves. It is her responsibility to have sex when and how he wants it. He proceeds until he has completed the act in a way that causes her major injuries. Now it is her fault for being whiny. Her lack of love caused him to express himself at work and lose his job without being paid.

Sadly, the ending of this story could be her death from physical injuries, suicide from the emotional trauma of helplessness, incarceration for assaulting this abuser while defending herself, or the death penalty for killing this offender.

For this survivor, she had been threatened numerous times and injured numerous times by this offender. Each time she tells herself that it will not be so bad when he gets home. He is a good husband most of the time.

She instantly becomes terrified as he begins the verbal abuse and hitting. She is emotionally and physically paralyzed. In her mind, there is no way that she could consider leaving because she would have no place to live and no income. Adversely, she does not realize that this has already happened.

College scenario—domestic violence. Let us add hope through a trauma-informed educator. This middle-aged survivor is taking classes at the local college while her husband is at work. She has called her instructor stating that she is sick, which seems to be happening more frequently now that her husband has lost his job. When this woman returns to class, the instructor notices a limp and small bruise on her face that is beginning to heal. This student seems to be avoiding the educator. The instructor recognizes theses clues and provides this student with a list of hotline numbers for sexual assault and domestic violence.

There are many directions in which this story can proceed. The best scenario is that the woman asks for the help of the instructor after glancing at the list of numbers. They sit down together and call the hotline. A domestic violence agency pays for a cab that takes the

survivor to a domestic violence shelter to begin a new life with noth-
ing from the past, expect her books, purse, and clothes that she is
wearing. Even with this apparently safe scenario, this woman typi-
cally will face the strong internal force or abuse bond that can pull
her back to this abuser.

Our scenarios now include returning to this abusive, violent man. He
is not always like this. True! She returns because things will get
better. True! The violence cycle includes periods of apology, kind-
ness, and heartfelt "I will not do this again."

She will learn to be a better wife, and he will stop abusing her. False!
The offender begins the abusive process of blaming repeatedly be-
cause that is what an offender does.

She returns because she sees no other choices, even with the informa-
tion provided at the shelter. Offenders create terror that bonds the
survivor. Leaving a violent relationship or situation has been documented as the most life-threatening time for the survivor. *The of-*
fender views this loss as abandonment and requires her to stay, no
matter what it takes. This cycle will not stop until help is added.

Returning to the offender will consist of a horrendous journey of
repeated abuse and sexual abuse. Hopefully, she can call 911. Or
having developed a safety plan while in the shelter, she grabs a small
bag of basic, necessary items such as keys, clothes, and important
papers of all nonoffending family members secreted by the door and
runs to a neighbor's home as prearranged. Together they can call a
domestic violence hotline for help.

When children are part of this family, each child needs an individual
safety plan that is age appropriate and includes their school supplies.
With domestic violence, leaving quickly will be necessary. Students
may not have time to get their school supplies, books, or homework.
Teachers often have additional supplies available. If an instructor
wants to be more involved, then discussing a safety plan individually
or as a class can be helpful. Asking a professional to provide informa-
tion can also be helpful if this is in the school policies and procedures.

Special Needs Population

Having sex with a person who is physically or emotionally unable to
understand about sexual behavior, how to say no, or what no means.
This special population deserves a book to encompass all the aspects of
safety and prevention. Everyone can learn.

Only two states, Nebraska and Nevada, had a reference to Americans with Disabilities Act (ADA) training programs within their department of education websites. Nebraska offered a seven-hour continuing education training specific to the ADA.[12]

Though the topic is about sexual abuse, this note seems important to add as a distinguishing factor about privacy vs voyeurism with a couple who are both physically disabled and sexually intimate. During a human sexuality master level course at University of Houston Clear Lake, a specific related need of persons with disabilities was noted. In order to be sexual, people with some types of physical disabilities frequently will require positioning in a safe environment by an attendant or caregiver. The caregiver or attendant will then provide privacy for the sexual intimacy of the couple after positioning.

> *Resources are available in the form of educational books sold in bookstores or found in school or public libraries. In addition, these books are especially helpful for persons who have learning challenges. There are a variety of learning levels available to match the need. Public libraries offer specific assistance and resources for teachers. Many age-appropriate educational books that include nude pictures can be utilized for learning about puberty and the body's normal growth and development.*
>
> *Other books will contain information about personal and relational sexual pleasure with pictures of people nude or in sexual positions. In distinguishing between sexually abusive pictures or photos without consent, these people have consented to be photographed for the pictures. Many books now utilize sketches or drawings rather than photos of people. Educational books are preferable to hidden publications used to provide sexual pleasure by children, youth, or adults. Students may use these hidden publications to learn about sexuality and their sexual organs.*
>
> *Consider the messages that are presented (i.e., secrecy, sexuality is forbidden, and sneaking is required to obtain information rather than open discussion and choice). Isolation is the core of sexual abuse. Young people and children using pornographic materials is sexual abuse.*
>
> *Hopefully, the distinguishing factor is that parents or adults are adding information about compassionate interactions with others while utilizing the educational books with children, youth, and adults to*

teach about sexuality and puberty. There are also age-appropriate curricula available at some schools.

Open Marriage Where One Person Has Not Consented

Open marriage means the spouse can participate in sexual behaviors with other people outside of the marriage.

Ritual Abuse or Cult Abuse

Grooming has occurred to honor the survivor for their participation in rituals that are dangerous and life endangering. These situations can be intergenerational from great-grandparents to grandparents to parents to children and are believed normal for the members. People are killed and tortured along with rampant sexual abuse among the families involving children, youth, and adults. The adult offenders would intermittently laugh at the pain of others while praising the survivor, who was forced to participate. When a child or person feels uncomfortable with the rituals, the survivor is threatened overtly or covertly. Several survivors noted having dental work done without anesthesia. Another was placed into an empty coffin for a time, while the parents and other adults thought this was entertaining.

Professional Use of Power

Having an authority, age, or influence difference between the survivor and the offender(s): church clergy, faith leaders, and priests have used their influence to sexually abuse children, youth, or adults. Again, the offender is responsible, not the survivor. One survivor spoke of reporting the sexual abuse by a religious leader and immediately was terrified. "They will come and get me and hurt me."

Professionals are ethically bound to provide services and education. A counselor, teacher, or other professional mixing sex or romance during their sessions or classes is sexual abuse. Report.

The professional needs to have skills of refusal for any client or student initiating romantic or sexual gestures. There have been instances where a student solicited a date or sex from a teacher. This is a serious concern, particularly with older students and younger teachers who may be close in age. Since the teacher will say "no," the student's behavior needs to be addressed. A student attempting to connect with a person in authority through a date or sex, may indicate past sexual abuse. If the teacher has sex with the student, the offender is the teacher. Both instances need to be reported.

Nude Beaches or Nude Communities Not Clearly Marked

There are many websites about nude beach etiquette. A nudist is to be clothed in parking lots, businesses that non-nudists may frequent, or any public area where clothed people are allowed.

Pornography

Pornography is taking pictures or looking at pictures of nude persons or persons in various sexual positions. Taking pictures of babies, children, or youth in this fashion is against the law. Taking sexual or nude pictures of adults without their permission is against the law.

Some people have found that they were being photographed during sexual interactions without their permission. This is sexual abuse. Please report this to the police. Decision making for children, youth, and even adults can be problematic without education.

One survivor found one parent's "stash" at three to four years old. This survivor craved looking at the pictures and "got caught" by the other parent. Now the pornographic pictures were forbidden fruit and were described in significance as "mother's milk." This survivor shared that discussing this childhood sexual abuse brought an anxious feeling even as an adult.

The incessant need to be stimulated by pictures drove a wedge between this survivor and the spouse. This adult survivor was unable to honor the boundary of no pornography requested by the spouse because of the obsession or pull to pornography. Pornography was easily found in dumpsters. Online this survivor could sign in "incognito." This demonstrates a repeated pattern beginning in early childhood.

Domestic violence within this marriage had escalated with verbal, emotional, and recently physical abuse by both people. The couple is now separated because of the violence, an emotional affair by the survivor, and previous isolation as a couple.

Picking up a sexual image was easier and more satisfying than the work required in relating to a person. The sexual abuse trauma of childhood will need to be addressed as this survivor learns to cope with life without pornography.

Witnessing Others Being Sexual

Some people seek witnesses during sex for sexual pleasure (exhibitionists). This is sexual abuse when the observers are children, teens, or nonconsenting adults. There is a difference between students viewing affectionate responses rather than overt sexual behaviors between adults. Viewing others during sexual behaviors may involve a lack of personal space within the home, the lack of planning for privacy, or the false belief that children, teens, or other adults are not affected. Many students talk openly with others about having the experience of viewing adults in a variety of sexual circumstances. When shared with an educator, this situation needs to be addressed. Listen and speak with the reporting agency, counselor, nurse, or the trauma team on campus. Social service referrals can be helpful with housing needs and boundary setting.

Hanging for Sexual Pleasure

Sexual stimulation is achieved by hanging oneself. This practice is meant to enhance sexual feelings during a period of asphyxiation or lack of oxygen. The results have often been loss of life. Self-hanging for sexual pleasure has killed many of our students.

Sadomasochism

Sadomasochistic practices involve attempting to heighten sexual pleasure by causing pain, injury, or lack of control with bondage or torture. There has been debate about sadomasochistic practices as abusive even with mutual consent.

Here is another perspective to be considered with respect to sadomasochistic practices. One survivor had used implements to injure the genital area while being sexual with self to create some feeling. This is not about discussing the moral aspects of masturbation. This survivor felt so numb that even gentle touch could not be felt. Many survivors note the lack of feeling or numbness physically and emotionally. This involves the need to inflict pain or injury due the numbing that has occurred from shutting down after being sexually abused.

Spanking

One National Abuse Hotline employee described a circumstance where a punishment would not be considered abuse or sexual abuse from a legal perspective. The situation was spanking a child once with the open palm of a hand on a child's clothed bottom as a form of punishment. Legally, this is allowed. Survivors of sexual abuse considered this practice of using a hand on their bottoms as sexual abuse, especially if their bottom was unclothed.

Survivors reported that their parents were often extremely angry and lost control during the punishment. The child was in fear and focused on what the punishment would entail or how bad the punishment would hurt. They had no idea or did not hear what they had done wrong.

Their parents spanked them with a belt, switch, or other implements multiple times, leaving marks on their body. If the punishment did include a parent's hand, the hand was used for multiple hits and often left marks on their bare back, bottom, or legs.

Therefore, the student became fearful, rather than understanding and making positive changes in their behavior. The underlying fear left this child vulnerable. Hitting or spanking usually leads to the loss of control of the disciplinarian during this sexual abuse.

One family member shared that the punishment of spanking was reserved for the male child, not female. Neither gender needs to be hit or spanked. Hitting or spanking does not work. "Hitting makes hitters," as quoted from a nurse practitioner.

Sexual Abuse of Animals—Bestiality

Children or youth may have participated in or witnessed adults being sexual with animals. The animal is unable to say "no." Therefore, this is sexual abuse of an animal.

These children, youth, or adults will need education and support about establishing boundaries to learn and change their behavior. Participating in sexual behavior with an animal is an offender behavior and is sexually abusive to the animal. The listening teacher or student may not be aware of this fact.

The Tennessee Department of Education has noted animal ethics on their website under agricultural business and finances. An animal has a right to not be abused in any form—physically or sexually.

BACKGROUND CHECKS

Several school districts noted the importance of background checks to assist with sexual abuse prevention. Alabama, Louisiana, Maryland, and New Hampshire were recognized on the state department of education websites for the background checks. The state of Pennsylvania recognized the need for background checks on nurses' aides who may work within the educational systems. Every employee of an educational setting needs to have a background check prior to hiring.

PROBLEM WITH NUMBERS

The author contacted a number that was thought to be the number to the state Family & Protective Services. This number (1-800-424-4453) was for a National Abuse Hotline for abuse support, not an agency for reporting abuse. There were counselors available to speak with anyone needing support 24/7.

The personnel of the National Abuse Hotline stated that they often received calls from persons thinking that they were calling their local abuse reporting system. Many times, the person was calling to ascertain whether the report needed to be made. The personnel provided information about each state and county abuse report lines. They also explained the laws related to sexual abuse reporting and could guide the caller. The personnel suggested to call in all reports because the reporter is "the voice of the child."

The staff of the National Abuse Hotline explained that some people did not call a report because they thought that Family & Protective

Services would separate the survivor from their family. Reporters were ambivalent about calling for this reason alone. The purpose of Family & Protective Services is to provide a safe environment for the survivor. This could mean a separation from the family for safety of the survivor.

The person who answered the phone indicated that each state can have different numbers to report abuse at the state level and other numbers for the county level. Noted was the confusion with so many phone numbers. Also mentioned was the lengthy delays in reaching a person to make a report. When the phone was answered, many times there would be a voice mail message to begin a report. The hotline personnel had been told that the official reporting hotline phone in some areas was never answered in some cases. This is not a workable solution.

Consequently, there is no national number to report abuse. Each state has its own numbers, which can be different at the state and county level. These numbers can be difficult to find. Reports of abuse are numerous and warrant a system that is easily accessible for reporters and manageable for those who work within the system.

The author had a disappointing experience calling a suicide hotline, with a lengthy wait and some delay noted from the employee in responding. Then, the phone made a weird sound and the call was ended. There was no return call. This demonstrates that more training or personnel may be needed.

LAMINATED REFERENCE CARD

Because there are extensive, confusing lists of resources and numbers for reporting, a laminated reference card is proposed. Plain pieces of paper can be laminated and cut to 3" × 5" or 4" × 6" size to place on each staff member's desk for review and easy reference. These may go in pockets or purses. Problems or suggestions are welcome to add to the usability of this idea.

REPORTING: 4 Ws—WHO, WHAT, WHEN, WHERE. LISTEN!! *Local number to call.*

SUICIDAL: "What are your plans to end your life? Where are the items?" Call 911.

BYSTANDER MOTIVATION: Talk to the survivor directly to see if they are all right. Tell the crowd that this behavior hurts and is violence. This needs to stop. Assign someone to call 911 if needed. Ask the crowd to disperse. Make a referral for the survivor.

COMMUNITY SEXUAL ABUSE PREVENTION AND RESOURCES

Every community has resources to educate, support, assist, and emphasize prevention related to sexual abuse. The focus is often for survivors, families, and their communities.

The following pages will present several sources of educational programs related to healing from sexual abuse and prevention. Many are nonschool based. As research continued, the sources were extensive and vast. Each source led to another. Currently, the internet seems to be our main directory for these programs. Many were found by word of mouth or through professionals who have made referrals, which may limit those in need from utilizing these wonderful programs.

How can we develop a national and worldwide directory of resources? Each agency or program is adding to the wealth of information independently.

SCHOOL-BASED PROGRAMS

State Department of Education School Programs for Sexual Abuse Prevention

Every state website was accessed informally once to compile this brief list of child sexual abuse prevention resources. When attempting to duplicate this research, I was often unable to find the same location. The university, college, training programs, home schooling, and other educational settings were not researched. There is an enormous resource pool available.

To begin to work together and expand our resources, is it possible to share these programs from state to state? Or is it more beneficial to have specific curricula and trainings that meet the needs of an individual state or district? Solutions often need a combination of both.

RESEARCH: FIFTY STATES AND THE DISTRICT OF COLUMBIA

District of Columbia[13]

This district has eleven departments of education that were not researched. The following program was noticed while viewing information on the District of Columbia website: Sextortion Prevention, Response, and Recovery into School EOP (Emergency Operations Plan) Planning by Charol Shakeshaft.

Alabama[14]

Background checks on every employee, specifically teachers
Education for students and staff regarding HIV/AIDS

Alaska[15]

Trauma engaged schools. Suicide awareness and response

Arizona[16]

Youth and mental health
First aid
AWARE with topics on substance abuse, mental health, and suicide

Arkansas[17]

Task force
Prevention through education

California[18]

Training and resources

Colorado[19]

Caring School Community—includes a fee to use
Internet protection in the library

Connecticut[20]

Statewide K–12 curriculum regarding sexual assault and abuse prevention program guidelines

Delaware[21]

Addiction

Florida[22]

First in 2019 to add a curriculum for K–12 about child trafficking pre-
vention
Sexual assault
Teen dating/violence
Comprehensive health education program with an elementary toolkit

Georgia[23]

Child abuse prevention resource manual, PowerPoint presentations,
and handouts
Suicide prevention model policy
Bullying prevention program

Hawaii[24]

Antibullying
Parent Project for ages eleven to twenty years

Loving solutions for ages five to ten years
Abuse and neglect
Family support Hawaii
Fatherhood program
Home visiting services
Parent toolkit

Idaho[25]

Keep Idaho students safe
Suicide prevention

Illinois[26]

Erin's Law Task Force General Assembly per PA96-1524 (May 2012)
Suicide prevention
Bullying
Harassment
Drug free schools

Indiana[27]

Child abuse prevention and response resources
Response policy and reporting procedures
Educational materials
Resources and school improvement topics to print
Sexual abuse education for kindergarten through twelfth grade
Corporations, charter schools, and accredited non-public schools required staff needs child abuse and neglect training every two years
Information for public, including parents and staff

Iowa[28]

Bullying
Harassment

Kansas[29]

Training program and tri state webinar Part 1 and Part 2 curriculum

Kentucky[30]

Bullying
Harassment
Training for child sexual abuse prevention

Louisiana[31]

Darkness to Light child sexual abuse program
Child advocacy program
Child abuse and neglect background checks for employees
Mandated reporting
Substance exposed newborn reporting
Safe sleep
Safe haven

Maine[32]

Health education prevention and response for suicide
Bullying
Model for child abuse prevention and response—all school personnel within six months of hire and every four years
Age appropriate classroom instruction

Maryland[33]

Child sex trafficking prevention and interventions
Education program on child sex trafficking
Background checks
Child abuse, neglect, and human trafficking
Employment history review for child abuse or child misconduct for public, nonpublic, contracting agencies

Massachusetts[34]

Comprehensive health curriculum framework K–12 violence prevention
Disease
First aid and CPR, safety, and injury prevention with how to handle verbal, physical, and emotional abuse
Tobacco, alcohol, and other substances education
Teen dating violence
Safe and supportive schools

Michigan[35]

Several articles were noted

Minnesota[36]

Bullying information
Erin's Law
Ensuring safe and supportive schools

Mississippi[37]

Health education contacts policy and resources
Health in action lesson plan
Love is abuse curriculum
Positive action
Lessons from literature for English teachers regarding physical, verbal, and sexual abuse
Parent information from birth to five years[38]

Missouri[39]

Antibullying
Student health and wellness
Training for mandated reporters for half-hour continuing education credit

Montana[40]

Information for school counselor
Article about LGBTQ concerns
Suicide prevention
VOICE: Violence prevention and support program (Montana State University VOICE Center provides support for survivors of sexual assault along with family, friends, and loved ones)[41]

Nebraska[42]

Antibullying
Preventing dating violence
Child labor laws information
Continuing education options:
Child abuse prevention training Safe with You
Getting down to business for caregivers
Home visitation training
Special Care seven-hour training for sensitivity to individuals with disabilities
Early learning guidelines from birth to five

Nevada[43]

ADA accessibility with articles regarding CPS
Teaching safety K–12
Women's substance abuse prevention and treatment
Sexual assault

New Hampshire.[44]

Criminal background checks
Childhood abuse and development
Sexual orientation
AOD: alcohol and other drugs with a middle school curriculum.

New Jersey[45]

Social and emotional learning
Resource manual for interventions and referrals
Educational outcomes for children who have had out of home placements
Frequently asked questions about sexual misconduct and child abuse

New Mexico[46]

Safe schools
Suicide prevention
Bullying prevention
Stop sexual assault in schools
Alcohol awareness
Huge list of resources/webinars/online courses
Options for parents and families

New York[47]

Spanish prevention resources
13833 results about child sexual abuse prevention

North Carolina[48]

Mission statements 1-2-3

North Dakota[49]

Resources/websites/online courses covering topics:
School shootings
Bullying prevention
Stop sexual assault in school
Alcohol awareness. Suicide prevention
Options for parents and families

Ohio[50]

Alcohol and sexual assault information
Safety and violence prevention curriculum
Module 4 handouts/resources/referrals
Teen sex trafficking for parents and educators

Oklahoma[51]

Youth violence
Professional development
Prevention resources
Health education
Bullying prevention
Hotline numbers

Oregon[52]

Child sexual abuse prevention
Sexual health promotion
Sexual violence protection, instruction strategies, and goals
School staff tip sheet

Pennsylvania[53]

SESAME-stop educator sexual abuse, misconduct, and exploitation
Key components of effective child sexual abuse prevention
Child exploitation awareness education
Recognizing and reporting misconduct under the educator discipline
act
Nurses' aid background checks and training

Rhode Island[54]

Sample reporting protocol for reporting child sexual abuse
Health and safety-students
Families
Great Schools

South Carolina[55]

Teens, students, and teachers
Active shooter resources
Substance abuse and prevention
Human trafficking resource

South Dakota[56]

A training guide for administration and educators addressing adult sexual misconduct in the school setting
Every Student Succeeds:
Child sexual abuse
Drug-free schools
Suicide
Bullying
Human trafficking
Violence prevention
Drug abuse
Harassment
Description of the use of Title II funds
Trauma-informed practices

Tennessee[57]

Laws
Safe Schools
Agricultural business and financial (animal ethics—right to not be abused)

Texas[58]

TEA: Texas Education Agency overview
Child sexual abuse.
Pregnancy and parenting
Human trafficking of school-aged children
Health and safe school environment of the coordinated school health model

Bullying
Cyber bullying

Utah[59]

Child sexual abuse prevention and information
Health education for students includes refusal skills and prohibiting electronic transmission of sexually explicit images
Health education prohibits information on teaching of premarital and extramarital relations, intercourse, stimulation, contraception, erotic behavior

Vermont[60]

Abuse, neglect, and exploitation registry
Mandatory reporting (Act 1 2009 and Act 60 2015) for principles, superintendents, headmasters, and educational staff
Online training available—only 30 percent had taken
All school employees, non-teaching staff, bus drivers, custodians, and food service staff
Vermont's Teachers Guide to Domestic and Sexual Violence: 1-800-649-5285 to report

Virginia[61]

VDOE prevention strategies and programs for child abuse and neglect
Guidelines for prevention of sexual mis conduct and abuse
Family life education
Human trafficking
Sexual harassment
Electronic use for sexual abuse education—352 sites

Washington[62]

Child sexual abuse prevention
HIV and sexual health education resources
Youth suicide prevention, intervention, and postvention

Commercial sexual exploitation and human trafficking
Trauma-informed school resources
Erin's Law
Health and safety
OSPI rulemaking agency—child sexual abuse prevention
Partners in education join forces against opioid epidemic

West Virginia[63]

Body safety education and sexual abuse prevention—developmentally appropriate toolkit (K–second, third–fifth, sixth–eighth, ninth–twelfth grades)
School personnel training
Expected behavior for safe and supportive schools
Toolkit for connecting social, emotional, and mental health

Wisconsin[64]

April is Sexual Assault Awareness and Child Abuse Prevention Month
Protecting children from sexual harm
Prevention and response to sexual violence in schools
Human trafficking and training information
School's role in preventing child abuse and neglect
Code of ethics for school nurses with information about signs and symptoms of sexual abuse, statistics, and other topics, such as human trafficking

Wyoming[65]

School safety summit in memo form
Child sexual abuse education, prevention, and response
Parent information
Trainings for personnel
Consult with federal, state, and local agencies to develop community-based strategies for health and safety programs that include:
Recognizing child sexual abuse
Personal boundaries

Violations
Grooming
Disclosure
Reducing self-blame
Mobilizing bystanders

Erin's Law is an important resource that has been noted on the above list. Erin's Law evolved from a childhood sexual abuse survivor who has developed information through a nonprofit organization available in most states. The information is for parents, teachers, children. Erin's Law involves curriculum, public speaking, resources, and training for lawyers.[66] Illinois, Minnesota, and Washington have this resource listed on their department of education websites.

Task forces have been formed to clarify and develop strategies to assist in sexual abuse prevention and support for survivors. The only state listed on the one-time review of the department of education website that noted task force was Arkansas.

PRISON-BASED PROGRAMS

New laws have been made to prevent rape in prison. Why is this important? Because an inmate who is in prison for a child sexual abuse offense or is suspected of having a same-gender sexual orientation is often raped while incarcerated, thus perpetuating the cycle of sexual abuse.

Hurt people, hurt people! Offenders being raped, especially in a prison setting, will not stop sexual abuse. Many prisoners who have a record of abusing others sexually have themselves been sexually abused as a child or youth. Thus continues the repetitive and perpetuating cycle of sexual abuse.

Within our legal system, the federally mandated Prison Rape Elimination Act (PREA) of 2003, which stipulates a zero-tolerance policy for staff- or inmate-initiated rape, was approved to address rape in prison. The need for this law indirectly implies that rape occurs frequently within the prison system.[67]

One survivor shared the experience of being in jail and prison. This woman stated that the PREA orientation was provided on the first day. There were posters throughout the prison regarding this law. She was in prison for injuring persons in another vehicle when she blacked out while driving. Her sexual abuse started at seven years old and lasted for several years. This survivor was in so much emotional pain from the childhood sexual abuse by her stepbrothers that a voice constantly told her to "Just do it. Get it over with." She attempted to suicide many times. Just prior to blacking out, she had injected an overdose of insulin with the purpose of suiciding. If the wreck had not occurred, she would have died without medical treatment.

Now she is alive to share her story. Within the prison system, there were courses on anger and stress management, with some sessions of cognitive behavioral therapy that she found useful. This survivor wondered whether, had there been prevention programs or trauma-informed teachers in her life when she was seven years old, suicide would have been an option. Suicidal thoughts and prison were direct aftereffects of her childhood sexual abuse.

The Prison Yoga Project is a trauma-informed program because offenders in prison have often been abused as children and adults. The Prison Yoga Project has been utilized at San Quentin State Prison and Los Colinas Detention Facility. This practice, guided by trained volunteers, confirms that offenders can change by addressing their personal traumas as well as the harm caused by their offending behavior.[68]

FAITH-BASED PROGRAMS

Many programs within faith-based communities have been established to inform students of all ages about their bodies, choices, safety, and well-being. Each program has special focuses within their curriculum. Please consider personal needs and preferences in choosing a program for your school campus or personal family. The point is that there are many nonschool-based programs within the community developed to support our children and adults in learning about boundaries and to assist in the prevention of sexual abuse through education.

The JACS (Jewish Alcoholics, Chemical Dependent Persons, and Significant Others) program was held in an addiction center prior to COVID-19 and offers a multitude of resources and support options.[69]

VIRTUS is one registered program that teaches about sexual abuse prevention within the Catholic church. Attending this presentation is required for all employees of a Catholic-based organization and available to students within Catholic schools.[70]

One teacher explained some details of this program. The teacher taught about how to recognize grooming, sexual abuse symptoms in peers, and internet safety. The class discussed offenders utilizing sexting and the internet to find people to hurt. The objective is to offend, not develop a relationship with an age-appropriate person. Instruction was also provided about the difference between full body hugs and partial hugs, such as an A-frame hug or side hug.

The teaching staff was told to never meet with a student alone or in a secluded area. Always talk privately with other people in sight and in public to avoid any compromising situations for the student or themselves as teachers.

The Harbor is a nondenominal faith community that has several programs directly or indirectly addressing sexual abuse. Embrace Grace is a thirteen-week program for women who are pregnant and not married. Embrace Life is for mothers after the baby's birth. The program was described by the contact person as a Christian-based, non-shaming mentoring-style parenting program. Embracing Life involves two semesters of ten weeks each. Embrace Grace has more than five hundred groups throughout the world in the United States, Australia, Canada, Ghana, Kenya, South Africa, and Uganda.[71]

Chains and Liberation is a program for women who have had previous sexual abuse, abandonment, or other abuses. Most have not shared this information with anyone previously. Another program is "Revive," for men and women with issues related to sex addiction.

Living Hope addresses unwanted approaches by persons of the same gender. This program is a six-week course that includes the person and their family.

Transform is an additional program sponsored at the Harbor. This program is a ministry for people who suffer with mental illness (depression, suicidal thoughts, or anxiety to name a few). A high percentage of attendees has experienced childhood sexual abuse.

Another resource is Love People, Not Pixels (LPNP), which discusses the concerns related to pornography. Grace Bible Church sponsors one program based in Houston, Texas.[72]

Anchor Point has three distinct programs related to pregnancy. One is Obria, a medical clinic for pregnancy. Hope Family Center offers parenting classes, spiritual counseling, and pregnancy resources. The third program is a private school called Excellent Minds Academy that has resources for autism and learning disabilities.[73]

Shelter from the Storm, coauthored by Cynthia Kubetin and James Mallory, is a private faith-based curriculum that is utilized by female sexual abuse survivors. While participating, survivors have a safe environment to share their stories, study, and have support within the group. This program is thirteen weeks in length with repetitive enrollment so the women can go deeper in learning more about themselves. The graduates help mentor the new attendees. Often, there is a waiting list to enroll. Everything is free other than the use of insurance for the medical care and counseling.[74]

Shelter from the Storm for victims of domestic violence is a program in California.[75]

In the late 1970s, the Methodist Church in Oklahoma offered several age-appropriate educational programs related to our bodies, boundaries, and sexuality. There was a program for each age group: preschool age, early school age, junior high–aged students, high school students, adults, and senior adults. Within each program, volunteers were trained to guide the attendees through the curriculum over a period of a few days. The child and youth programs included time within the curriculum for the parents to meet separately with the leaders. At the end, the children and parents shared about their participation in a structured way as part of the curriculum.

AGENCY PROGRAMS

The Montrose Center of Houston offers a multitude of resources including a sexual assault program for people within the LGBT community. The center provides sources for survivors related to counseling, case management, court and hospital support, protective orders, advocacy, and attorneys who are trauma informed about the needs of the LGBT community in Harris County and the surrounding counties. SPRY is another program developed specifically for senior adults over 60 whose sexual orientation is LGBT. The Montrose Center participates in the Gay Student Alliances and provides safe zones with therapists within the school system. LGBT survivors in prison can receive assistance through the Montrose Center under the Prison Rape Elimination Act. Domestic violence, assault, hate crimes, and human trafficking are types of abuse that the Montrose Center addresses.

Students as early as the age of six may recognize the need to change genders. Though these programs are for a little older students, the Montrose Center has two programs available. The first is Hatch for those students thirteen to twenty-one years old and Hatchling for students who are eight to thirteen years old.[76]

The Houston Area Women's Center aids persons in heterosexual relationships.[77]

Unbound Houston and Unbound Global are programs established to educate about human trafficking. These two programs provide information for survivors, concerned persons, and professional training for schools or organizations. The survivor line (346-202-4299) is open 24/7. One of their programs, Keeping Students Safe, is currently used in the Texas school system.[78]

The Sexual Assault Resource Center in Bryan, Texas has a twenty-four-hour hotline (979-731-1000). There are counseling, education, outreach, crisis intervention, volunteer, and internship opportunities.[79]

SNAP Survivors Network of those Abused by Priests: twenty-one states are listed with resource numbers to report or discuss abuse. There is information for survivors and advocates.[80]

ADDICTION-BASED PROGRAMS

For persons who are survivors of sexual abuse or offenders who are open to finding help, twelve-step programs are founded on spiritual solutions and are available throughout the world. These are based on the twelve steps, twelve traditions, twelve concepts, and principles of Alcoholics Anonymous.

Open and closed is a criterion for attending. Open meetings are available to professionals and other interested persons. Please respect the concept of anonymity, which means not disclosing who is in the meeting or what they shared. Closed meetings are reserved only for those persons who think that they may have a problem.

Twelve-step–based programs often provide information for family, friends, and professionals who are concerned and want to learn more.

Please research additional twelve-step groups for any specific topics of interest. Following is a list of a few related programs.

- AA (Alcoholics Anonymous[81])
- Al-Anon and Alateen (Al-Anon for family and friends, Alateen for teens)[82]
- ABA (Anorexics and Bulimics Anonymous)[83]
- COSA (for persons affected by compulsive sexual behavior)[84]
- GA (Gamblers Anonymous)[85]
- ISA (Infidelity Survivors Anonymous)[86]
- NA (Narcotics Anonymous)[87]
- OA (Overeaters Anonymous)[88]
- PAA (Porn Addicts Anonymous) [89]
- SAA (Sex Addicts Anonymous)[90]
- SIA (Survivors of Incest Anonymous)[91]
- SLAA (Sex and Love Addicts Anonymous)[92]
- Sexworkers Anonymous[93]
- VA (Violence Anonymous)[94]

By utilizing the phone, Zoom, Skype, and other types of virtual meetings, many twelve-step–based programs have continued to provide support while in-person meetings have been suspended due to COVID-19. Exploring and making referrals to these worldwide resources can be immensely helpful.

The twelve-step programs address sexual abuse openly with the term *thirteenth stepping*. There is no thirteenth step. This term means that a person who has attended meetings for a while approaches a new person for sex or personal relationship. These support groups are not meant for sexual hookups or curiosity.

Members are usually encouraged to wait for an extended time to begin building a romantic relationship. People share their phone numbers within the fellowship for support, nonromantic fellowship, and sponsorship. Early relationships are discouraged; *thirteenth stepping* is not accepted or condoned.

BOY SCOUTS

Sadly, our school system and many other organizations can be affected by offenders. In February 2020, news reports related that the Boy Scouts organization had filed for bankruptcy due to reports and legal action expenses regarding alleged sexual abuse. There have also been media reports of male and female offenders within our schools. No organization is exempt.

PROPOSALS

- Mandate school training *yearly* prior to the beginning of school for all school staff, even non-teaching staff, about reporting any abuse (sexual abuse). For new employees, another mandated training can be added during the year.
- Provide continuing educational credits for administrators, teachers, and school related professionals. This would include all the different professionals providing services on the school campus.
- Mandate reporters to work with other staff in making reports. This would be necessary if a non-mandated employee or person were the person to hear the Outcry. Mandated staff could sit with the listener while a report is made. Or the listening person and the survivor can be referred to a mandated employee, such as the school nurse, counselor, principal, or vice principal. The original listener, whether mandated or non-mandated, needs to make a report.
- Create a committee to review, consolidate, and establish a national resource panel of information, abuse, and sexual abuse prevention programs, and resources that can be utilized by all fifty states.
- Establish a task force, organization, or committee to compile all national hotline numbers.
- Provide one national number for reporting all abuse and sexual abuse.
- Organize a trauma-informed team at each school that can immediately be available to assist any teacher during an Outcry, Response, or the reporting process. This team needs to have immediate communication to assign a trauma-informed staff member to the classroom in the interim.

- Laminate 3" × 5" or 4" × 6" cards with 911, the local report number to call, what to say, and the 4Ws for abuse, sexual abuse, and suicidal thought/plan reporting. This card should be at each desk, including teachers, administration, counselors, nurses, principals, assistant principals, volunteers, and non-teaching staff.
- Refer the survivor to tutoring, counseling, and other support programs. Confidentiality is vital! Reports are not to be discussed by personnel other than with the survivor or reporter(s) involved. This is the reason that offenders or survivors are not identified on an educator's student list.
- Implement referral sources for the listener/reporter, such as employee assistance programs, counseling, or other types of support off campus.
- Develop school, community, counseling, and support programs for male survivors.
- Fund and establish translation resources with a base of worldwide languages for immediate needs.
- Record the primary languages of all the students, families, and employees at each educational setting.

#GraduateTogether, America Honors the High School Class of 2020.[95] Domestic violence, racism, financial illiteracy, forced early marriages, lack of education for females, homelessness, street violence, and special needs were recognized as major concerns. The fact that these graduating seniors are aware and speaking of these critical events demonstrates positive change. Similar concerns from over thirty years ago were observed and noted within this book.

Awareness is the beginning of change. Awareness is validated by open communication about sexual abuse and prevention, compassionate recognition of the long term affects of sexual abuse, focusing on survivor needs with dedicated services, practicing trauma-informed concepts and skills in the classroon and on campus, and new laws addressing sexual abuse such as mandated reporting, Title IX,[96] and the Prison Rape Elimination Act. *Outcry Response* provides a guide for educators, administrators, students, families, and communities to work together to create and share solutions for compassionately responding to Outcries of sexual abuse.

NOTES

1. https://metoomvmt.org.
2. COVID-19 Special, April 3, 2020 at 7:00 p.m. on KHOU 11.
3. https://www.fbi.gov/video-repository/newss-what-is-sextortion/view. Call the FBI (1-800-225-5324).
4. https://www.sexhelp.com/about-iitap.
5. https://stepupprogram.org/topics/hazing/; https://www.colorado.edu/ova/examples-hazing.
6. https://www.psychologytoday.com/us/basics/gaslighting; https://www.psychologytoday.com/us/blog/here-there-and-everywhere/201701/11-warning-signs-gaslighting.
7. http://www.montrosecenter.org/hatch-youth.
8. OK, Inc. Friends4Friends Campaign. https://operationkeepsake.com/students/friends-4-friends-campaign/. Another documentary from OK, Inc.'s Friends4Friends was *Sexting—Reckless Revenge*.
9. https://www.uscis.gov/humanitarian/forced-marriage; https://www.theahafoundation.org/forced-marriage.
10. https://en.wikipedia.org/wiki/Forced_marriage.
11. https://definitions.uslegal.com/s/sexual-misconduct/.
12. https://www.ada.gov.
13. https://www.ed.gov/category/location/district-columbia.
14. https://www.alsde.edu.
15. https://education.alaska.gov.
16. https://www.azed.gov.
17. https://portal.arkansas.gov.
18. https://www.cde.ca.gov.
19. http://www.cde.state.co.us/.
20. https://portal.ct.gov.
21. https://www.doe.k12.de.us/.
22. http://www.socflorida.com/.
23. https://www.gadoe.org/Pages/Home.aspx.
24. http://www.hawaiipublicschools.org/.
25. https://www.idaho.gov.
26. https://www.isbe.net.
27. https://www.doe.in.gov.
28. https://www.educateiowa.gov.
29. https://www.ksde.org/.
30. https://education.ky.gov/Pages/default.aspx.
31. https://www.louisianabelieves.com/.
32. https://www.maine.gov.

33. www.marylandpublicschools.org.
34. https://www.doe.mass.edu/.
35. https://www.michigan.gov/mde.
36. https://mn.gov/portal/
37. https://www.mdek12.org/.
38. https://www.futureswithoutviolence.org/.
39. https://mo.gov.
40. https://mt.gov/education/.
41. http://www.montana.edu/oha/voice/. VOICE Center 24-Hour Confidential Support Line.
42. https://www.education.ne.gov.
43. http://www.doe.nv.gov/.
44. https://www.education.nh.gov/.
45. https://www.nj.gov/education.
46. https://webnew.ped.state.nm.us.
47. http://www.nysed.gov/.
48. https://stateboard.ncpublicschools.gov.
49. https://www.nd.gov/dpi/.
50. http://education.ohio.gov/.
51. https://sde.ok.gov.
52. https://www.oregon.gov/ode/.
53. https://www.education.pa.gov/.
54. https://www.ride.ri.gov/.
55. https://www.ed.sc.gov.
56. https://www.doe.sd.gov.
57. https://www.tn.gov.
58. https://tea.texas.gov/.
59. https://schools.utah.gov.
60. https://education.vermont.gov.
61. https://www.doe.virginia.gov.
62. https://www.K12.wa.us.
63. https://wvde.us.
64. https://dpi.wi.gov.
65. https://edu.wyoming.gov.
66. www.erinslaw.org.
67. https://www.ojp.gov/program/programs/prisonrapeelimination; https://www.prearesourcecenter.org/about/prison-rape-elimination-act-prea.
68. https://prisonyoga.org.
69. https://www.addictioncenter.com/treatment/support-groups/jewish-alcoholics-chemically-dependent-persons-and-significant-others-jacs/.
70. https://www.virtusonline.org/.

71. https://embracegrace.com/.
72. https://www.gbchouston.org/lovepeoplenotpixels.
73. https://www.facebook.com/excellentmindsacademy.
74. https://www.amazon.com/Shelter-Storm-Survivors-Sexual-Abuse/dp/1515030237.
75. https://www.yelp.com/biz/houston-area-womens-center-houston-2; https://www.shelterfromthestorm.com/who-we-are/.
76. http://www.montrosecenter.org/;https://www.usatoday.com/news/education/; https://www.hrc.org/resources/establishing-an-allies-safe-zone-program; https://www.childwelfare.gov/topics/preventing/prevention-programs/schoolbased.
77. https://hawc.org/.
78. https://www.unboundhouston.org; https://www.unboundnow.org.
79. https://www.sarcbv.org.
80. https://www.snapnetwork.org.
81. https://aa.org.
82. https://al-anon.org/al-anon-meetings.
83. https://aba12steps.org.
84. https://cosa-recovery.org/.
85. http://www.gamblersanonymous.org/ga/.
86. http://www.isurvivors.org.
87. https://na.org.
88. https://oa.org.
89. https://pornaddictsanonymous.org.
90. https://saa-recovery.org.
91. https://siawso.org.
92. https://slaafws.org.
93. https://sexworkersanonymous.webs.com.
94. http://violenceanonymous.org.
95. https://www.graduatetogether2020.com (aired at 7:00 p.m. May 16, 2020 on several TV channels).
96. https://titleix.harvard.edu/what-title-ix.

RESOURCES

As I researched the topic of sexual abuse, I discovered an enormous list of resources, leading to the dilemma of what to include. I compiled this list from suggestions of the interviewees. Many authors have written several books related to this topic, with only a few referenced here. The noted resources are not by my preference or listed by importance. Several local resources are noted for the purpose of informing.

Not all resources noted in the text are listed here.

Please feel free to research topic areas of interest that are supplemental to this list.

Child Protective Services for Texas only: 1-800-252-5400 or www.txabusehotline.org.
Adult Protective Services for Texas only: 1-800-252-5400 or www.txabusehotline.org.
SAAFE HOUSE https://www.saafehouse.org, Huntsville, Texas.
Gay and Lesbian Switchboard. TEXAS only resources: 713-529-3211.
National GLBT Hotline: 888-234-3211.
Sexual Assault of Boys and Men: 877-628-1466 or lin6.org
National Domestic Violence Hotline: 800-799-7233 or thehotline.org
National Human Trafficking Hotline: 888-373-7888 (TTY: 711) Text 233733 or humantraffickinghotline.org

BOOKS

Allender, Dan B. *The Wounded Heart: Hope for Adult Victims of Childhood Sexual Abuse*. Colorado Springs, CO: NavPress, 1990.

Bancroft, Lundy. *When Dad Hurts Mom: Helping Your Children Heal the Wounds of Witnessing Abuse*. New York: Penguin, 2004.

Bass, Ellen, and Laura Davis. *Beginning to Heal: A First Book for Men and Women Who Were Sexually Abused as Children*. New York: Quill, HarperCollins, 1993.

Bass, Ellen, and Louis Thornton. *I Never Told Anyone: Writings by Women Survivors of Child Sexual Abuse*. New York: HarperCollins, 1991.

Bauer, Wolfgang. *Stolen Girls: Survivors of Boko Haram Tell Their Story*. New York: New Press, 2017. United States. Translated by New Press, 2017. Berlin: Suhrkamp Verlg, 2016.

Brown, Brene. *Men, Women and Worthiness: The Experience of Shame and the Power of Being Enough*. Louisville, CO: Sounds True, 2012.

Byers, Ann. *Confronting Violence Against Women: Sexual Assault and Abuse*. New York: Rosen Publishing, 2016.

Coles, Kim. *I'm Free, But, It'll Cost You: The Single Life According to Kim Coles*. New York: Hyperion, 1997.

Craig, Susan E. *Trauma-Sensitive Schools for the Adolescent Years: Promoting Resiliency and Healing Grades 6–12*. New York and London: Teachers College, Columbia University, 2017.

Davis, Laura. *Allies in Healing: When the Person You Love Was Sexually Abused as a Child*. New York: HarperCollins, 1991.

———. *Courage to Heal*. 20th Anniversary Edition. New York: Harper-Collins, 2008.

———. *Courage to Heal Workbook for Women and Men Survivors of Child Sexual Abuse*. New York: HarperCollins, 1990.

Divakaruni, Chitra Banerjee. *Arranged Marriage*. New York: Anchor Books. Doubleday, 1995.

Edmondson, Sarah. *Scarred: The True Story of How I Escaped NXIVM, the Cult that Bound My Life*. San Francisco: Chronicle Prism, 2019.

Gray, Roxanne, ed. *Not That Bad: Dispatches from Rape Culture*. New York: HarperCollins, 2018.

Griffin, Misty. *Tears of the Silenced: An Amish True Crime Memoir of Childhood Sexual Abuse, Brutal Betrayal, and Ultimate Survival*. Miami, FL: Mango Publishing, 2018.

Haley, Alex. *Roots: The Saga of an American Family*. New York: Dell, Inc. 1976.

Holmes, Patricia Hunt. *Searching for Pilar*. Plano, TX: River Grove Books, 2018.

Jennings, Jazz. *Being Jazz. My Life as a (Transgender) Teen*. Listening Library. Penguin Random House, 2016. Also available in print.

Jones, Dawn Scott. *When a Woman You Love Was Abused: A Husband's Guide to Helping Her Overcome Childhood Sexual Molestation*. Grand Rapids, MI: Kregel Publications, 2012.

Lew, Michael. *Victims No Longer: The Classic Guide for Men Recovering from Child Sexual Abuse*. 2nd ed. New York: HarperCollins, 2004.

Lloyd, Rachel. *Girls Like Us: Fighting for a World Where Girls Are Not for Sale, an Activist Finds Her Calling and Heals Herself*. New York: HarperCollins, 2011.

Love 146. *Not A Number: A Child Trafficking and Exploitation Prevention Curriculum*. 2nd ed. New Haven, CT, 2014, 2017.

McGibbon, Kathy. *Destined: The Unspoken Revealed*. Self-published, 2015.

Neff, Kristin. *Self-Compassion: The Proven Power of Being Kind to Yourself*. New York: HarperCollins Publishers, 2011.

Palfy, Kelli. *MeN Too: Unspoken Truths About Male Sexual Abuse*. Edmonton, Alberta: Peaks & Valleys Publishing, 2020.

Rosenberg, Marshall. *Nonviolent Communication: A Language of Life*. 3rd ed. Encinitas, CA: Puddle Dancer Press, 2015.

Schwartz, Arielle. *The Complex PTSD Workbook: A Mind-Body Approach to Regaining Emotional Control and Becoming Whole*. Berkley, CA: Althea Press, 2016.

Seigel, Daniel J., and Marion F. Solomon, eds. *Healing Trauma: Attachment, Mind, Body, and Brain*. New York and London: Norton, 2003.

Smith, Linda. *Renting Lacy: A Story of America's Prostituted Children*. Vancouver, WA: Shared Hope International, 2013.

Van der Kolk, Bessel. *The Body Keeps the Score: Brain, Mind, and Body in the Healing of Trauma*. New York: Penguin, 2014.

Walker, Alice. *The Color Purple*. New York: Pocket Books, 1982.

————. *You Can't Keep A Good Woman Down*. New York, London: Harcourt Brace and Company, 1981.

Walker, Mekisha. *But, Why Did You Stay? How I Survived Domestic Violence*. USA: Mekisha Jane Walker, 2020.

Walsh, Julia, and Natalie Garnett MacDonald. *Surviving "The Life:" How I Overcame Sex Trafficking*. London: Unbound, 2018.

Wilson, Gary. *Your Brain on Porn: Internet Pornography and the Emerging Science of Addiction*. United Kingdom: Commonwealth Publishing, 2014. 2nd ed. 2017.

Yowell, Alisha. *Doubt Thou the Stars Are Fire*. New York: Xlibris, 2019.

LIBRARY REFERENCES

Some public libraries have a special online reference section specifically for teachers. Please ask the librarian at your educational institution or public library for information.

Klor, Ellin, and Sarah Lapin. *Serving Teen Parents: From Literacy to Life Skills*. Libraries Unlimited Professional Guide for Young Adult Libraries Series. Santa Barbara, CA: Libraries Unlimited, 2011.

Luginbuehl, Marsha, and Val Chadwick Bagley. *Settle for No More Bullying, Harassment, or Abuse!* Self-published, 2019. Anti-Victim questionnaire and Happy Relationship questionnaire are included.

SOCIAL MEDIA

Hendricks, David. "Mind Is Everything." YouTube. TEDx Transverse City, https://www.youtube.com/watch?v=xI8lLpYtQ6M&t=845s.

Podcasts

Cosby, other offenders, and survivors.

WEBSITES

Crime Victim Services. Lutheran Community Services for Clark County, Vancouver, WA, and Multnomah County, Portland, OR. https://lcsnw.org.

Donna Clark Love. Website www.bullyingexpert.org. Bullying Educator | Speaker | Trainer | Expert.

Magpies & Peacocks. https://magpiesandpeacocks.org. Go to menu. Select MAKR COLLECTIVE for survivor resources. LBGTIA friendly. Nonprofit Design House 501(c)3.

National Coalition of Anti-Violence Programs (NCAVP). https://www.nsvrc.org/organizations/71.

National Coalition of Anti-Violence Programs NYC. https://avp.org/ncavp/.

RAINN Rape, Abuse, Incest National Hotline. https://www.rainn.org.

Sexual Assault of Boys and Men. https://1in6.org.

Texas Association Against Sexual Assault. https://www.facebook.com/taasa.

Texas Council on Family Violence. https://nnedv.org/meet-texas-council-family-violence/.

PLAYS

Eyen, Tom. *Dreamgirls*. Performance at Shadow Creek High School Pearland, Texas in February, 2020.

Kaufman, M. J. *Sensitive Guys*. Performed at Stages in Houston, August 15–23, 2020 on Zoom.

MUSIC AND SONGS

Use the internet to look up songs about incest, domestic violence, rape, human trafficking, sexually abused children, and other topics related to sexual abuse. Listed are only a few.

Barletta, Gino Maurice, Scott Bruzenak, Mike Campbell, Britten New-bill, songwriters. Daya, singer. *Sit Still, Look Pretty*. Kobalt Music Publishing LLC, Warner Cappell Music, Inc. BMG Rights, 2019.

Caracciolo, Alessia, Andrew Wansel, Coleridge Tillman, Warren Felder, songwriters. *You're Beautiful*. Sony/ATV Music Publishing LLC, Universal Music Publishing Group, 2016.

Jerkins, Fred, III, Kelendria Rowland, Lashawn Ameen Daniels, Rodney Jerkins, Beyoncé Knowles, Latavia Roberson, Letoya Luckett, songwriters. *Survivor*. Warner Chappell Publisher, 2001.

Knowles, Beyoncé, and Kenneth Fambro. *The Story of Beauty*. London: Beyoncé Publishing, 2001.

Perrin, Freddie, Fekaris, Dino, writers. Gaynor, Gloria, singer. *I Will Survive*. United States: Polydor Records, 1978.

Pulse, Steel. Mass Manipulation (album). *Human Trafficking*. Canada: Rezz, 2017.

JOURNALS

Minahan, Jessica. "Making School a Safe Place." *Educational Leadership* 77, no. 2 (October 2019): 30–35.

ABOUT THE AUTHOR

Kathleen Davis has an array of licenses and education that provide the insight and experience for *Outcry Response*. She is a registered nurse, licensed professional counselor, and licensed chemical dependency counselor and is certified with the National Board of Certified Counselors. She has been a certified family life educator.

Through the College of Education, she has earned a master of arts and a master of science degree in counseling. In private practice, she worked primarily with people who have experienced childhood sexual abuse. She has utilized psychodrama and art therapy with a trauma-informed approach.

Ms. Davis has developed a schoolwide health program and presented on sex addiction, suicide, depression referencing the geriatric depression scale, sexually transmitted diseases, hepatitis, HIV/AIDS, sexual abuse, school-based abuse reporting procedures, and senior adult sexuality. She has organized health fairs and worked with adults and adolescents on psychiatric units and with the geriatric community.

Ms. Davis has volunteered at a domestic violence shelter, a drug rehab home for women, homeless day center, Planned Parenthood, and the Methodist Church Human Sexuality Program for junior high school students and their parents. She worked in palliative care and guest relations, as an interim director and lead case manager at Catholic Charities Senior Services, a charge nurse in nursing homes, and a case manager with hospice.

www.ingramcontent.com/pod-product-compliance
Lightning Source LLC
Chambersburg PA
CBHW020004290326
41935CB00007B/305